Wrestling the Hulk

LINDA

wm

WILLIAM MORROW
An Imprint of HarperCollins*Publishers*

HOGAN

Wrestling the Hulk

My
Life
Against
the
Ropes

Insert photographs are courtesy of the author.

HarperCollins books may be purchased for educational, business, or sales
promotional use. For information please write: Special Markets Department, HarperCollins Publishers, 10 East 53rd Street, New York, NY
10022.

FIRST EDITION

Designed by Jamie Lynn Kerner

Library of Congress Cataloging-in-Publication Data has been applied for.

ISBN 978-0-06-203020-7

10 11 12 13 14   DIX/QG   10 9 8 7 6 5 4 3 2 1

CONTENTS

Prologue   vii

Chapter 1:   California Dreams   1

Chapter 2:   Two Blondes Walk into a Bar . . .   22

Chapter 3:   Ringside   40

Chapter 4:   Coast to Coast   58

Chapter 5:   Oh Baby!   76

Chapter 6:   The Other Woman   94

Chapter 7:   Guilty Pleasures   112

Chapter 8:   Going Through the Motions   123

Chapter 9:   Welcome to Miami   144

Chapter 10:   The Liar's Den   162

Chapter 11:   End of an Era   185

Chapter 12:   Cougar Unleashed   204

Epilogue   233

Acknowledgments   235

PROLOGUE

 AM DIGGING. THE GROUND IS HARD. THE DIRT IS heavy. I keep pushing forward with my shovel, digging deeper and deeper and deeper. But this is nothing new to me. I've been digging myself out of holes my entire life, and I've played many roles while doing it. Linda Hogan, wife of the wrestling icon Hulk Hogan. Linda Hogan, mother to Brooke and Nick Hogan. Linda Hogan, television personality. And now Linda Hogan, *farmer*?

Yes, sir. I am standing in a ditch at my avocado farm in California, Sunny Girl Avocados. My newest role is a reminder of my freedom. When you endure the public and private battles I have and survive, you're lucky to be the one holding the shovel! And it's not a coincidence that I am growing avocados. They have one of the thickest skins of any fruit, and early on I learned the importance of having a thick skin.

Since the divorce became final two years ago, people have often asked me when I was going to tell my side of the story. Friends, family, colleagues, and even strangers on the street would come up to me and ask what *really* happened. I was married to an icon, and I was fiercely loyal to him and to my children. Then, after the two decades we spent building an empire together, that empire crumbled. The family that was my life force for so long seemed to be taken away in a flash. My husband was gone. My son was in jail. My daughter lived in Miami. The ensuing divorce battle has now become Hollywood folklore.

It took a long time for me to realize that I needed to leave. Or maybe he just wanted me to leave. Either way, I knew that I had to make a decision and probably face the battle of my life.

Sure, I had access to the media to tell my story as the divorce was unfolding, but I never took advantage of it. I was dealing with Hulk Hogan, somebody with a huge ego. Somebody who doesn't like losing at anything. He shot back at me in the media when I wasn't even shooting in the first place. *If you let the fire smolder, it will eventually go out*, I thought. I knew that there would come a time when it would need to be discussed publicly. That time has come. That time is now.

It's the end of the day. The sun begins to set with deep gold and orange tones across the mountains. I put down my shovel and sit on a rock after an honest day's work. *Honest* is an interesting choice of words. My husband wasn't being honest in our marriage, and it was time for me to be honest with myself. This is my story, an honest account of my life that I hope will offer others inspiration to move on in their own lives in a more positive way. I was forced to learn these lessons the hard way, but as the saying goes, "Without the lows, the highs wouldn't be so incredible." Now that I've had my hardships,

I am much more grateful for the new doors God has opened for me.

I hope this book will help you learn from my mistakes and find all the joys I found once I summoned the courage to take the first step toward happiness.

Wrestling the Hulk

Chapter One

CALIFORNIA DREAMS

ERRY GENE BOLLEA, AKA WRESTLER HULK Hogan—born in Tampa, Florida, Thunderlips in *Rocky III*—this was the guy I would end up spending my life with, I thought. After a stormy divorce from Terry that for two years served as a platform of entertainment and drama for the tabloids, our marriage was over. I've seen myself through a lot of things, but this was something that I thought I would never have to face. In retrospect, the reality of this happening was the hardest thing I have ever had to go through in my life personally and publicly. Starting over again at fifty has been life-changing, an uphill climb, and a test of endurance. It was my choice to move on, ditch the drama, and start living again.

I needed to start my whole life over and I needed to be with my family on the West Coast for a while. California has always been my real home, but I ended up staying in Florida full-time until the divorce was settled. Another arrow in my heart. While distance from Terry would've been nice, I stayed strong during the two years when my divorce was tried. And when it was all over, I was finally able to spend some time in the place I loved.

California, here I come. Surf's up, bitches!

As I've spent more time here again, I feel like the old Linda. Actually, I feel like a young Linda—the one who doesn't just live life, but *lives* to live life. Family has always been such an important thing to me, and my parents have set a solid example. They have stayed together through thick and thin and just celebrated their fifty-second wedding anniversary.

IN 1957, MY MOTHER, GAIL, MET MY FATHER, JOE, IN THE GRAND-stands of Hollywood High. My mom was in tenth grade and my dad was a senior. There was an immediate attraction between the young couple. My mom said my dad looked like James Dean. And he proved to be a rebel *with* a cause: to offer my mom a better life.

Dad came from a big, warm family with an older brother and a younger sister. His father was a police officer and his mother, a nurse. My paternal grandfather was German and English, and my grandmother was a full-blooded Swede. My father's side of the family were all blonds, so obviously I look like them, but I definitely get my energetic personality from my Italian mom.

My mother's grandparents came from Italy to the United

States for a better life. After my grandfather sold his share in an Italian market he owned with his brother in Michigan, they settled right in the heart of Hollywood, California, on Sunset Boulevard and Highland Avenue. Since my grandfather (whom I never knew) understood the grocery business well, he got a job working at Ralphs, which would eventually become a popular chain of supermarkets on the West Coast.

Just as infidelity would eventually take its toll on my marriage to Terry, it also affected my family several generations prior. My grandfather ended up having an affair with a woman who was a cashier at Ralphs. My grandmother was not only devastated but also torn. While Hollywood marriages come and go, back then if you were Catholic, it was almost unheard of to get a divorce. However, the faith that my grandmother had in my grandfather had been destroyed. It was impossible for her to save the marriage.

My grandmother got divorced and eventually landed a job at Bank of America to support her two young children. Often, my great-grandmother would watch the children during the day while my grandmother was at work. My great-grandmother was used to the old country in Italy where children had more freedom to run and play. However, this was Hollywood—a whole different world. One afternoon, tragedy struck. My great-grandmother was watching my mom's four-year-old sister, Linda (whom I was named after). She was playing in an alleyway where the delivery trucks would go. A delivery truck was parked nearby, and Linda played in a planter by its back bumper. The driver got in and never saw Linda. He put the truck into reverse, and accidentally ran over Linda and killed her.

This horrific accident sent the family and my mother into

an even more difficult phase of their lives. My mom became a latchkey kid and attended nine schools in twelve years. When she met my father, his normal upbringing and solid family unit were a breath of fresh air. She was longing for a stable family life and was strongly drawn to him.

My mom married my dad when she was seventeen and he was nineteen, which was not unusual for that era. Almost immediately after they got married, my mom got pregnant. I was their first child, and I was born on August 24, 1959. My dad went off to serve in the army and was stationed in Texas. During the first two years of my childhood, I didn't see much of him. My parents were devoted to each other and to their new little family. They had so little financially, yet they had so much dedication in their marriage.

I dreamed of one day having a marriage like the one my parents had. They have always had a mutual respect for each other. Sure it was stressful with my father working to support three children, but my mom had this uncanny ability to always see the glass as half full. They genuinely loved each other, and I think that has helped them weather many storms. My mother was very attached to having a family because she grew up without one. She swore she would do things differently, and she did. I think her influence of not dwelling on the negative in the marriage and the ability to keep turning to the next page in life helped me stay in my marriage with Terry for over two decades.

My mom and dad presented a united front when it came to us kids. As my marriage to Terry evolved into us raising children, I have always wished that we would have had the same mindset that my parents did. Instead, I was always the disciplinarian and he was always the good guy. Whenever I had to reprimand the kids, Terry would mock me behind my back as if he was one of the kids, too. This made me out to be even *more* of a bad guy than I really was. Even when he knew my decision was the right one, and better for the kids, safer or whatever, he'd still go against me, mimicking me and starting arguments between us. Even if it wasn't the right thing to do for the kids, he just loved pushing my buttons, confusing the kids and trying to be the *cool* parent, so he could win the "popularity contest." If I said black, he said white.

Kids need parents to maintain a united front. It shouldn't be the parents' priority to be their kids' friends first. They have friends at school. It really made it so hard for me, trying to rear them with his senseless game playing and button pushing, that I frequently wished my marriage could've been more like the one my parents had. No matter what happened when I was growing up, if I was in trouble, my mother backed my dad up and vice versa, regardless of whether either parent was right or wrong.

WHEN MY DAD GOT OUT OF THE ARMY, MY MOM, DAD, AND I MOVED back to California. We settled in North Hollywood. Within that first year, my younger sister, Christie, was born. She was a shy, skinny, towheaded girl, and I welcomed her company. But before she turned four months old, my mother announced that she was already pregnant again! Nine months later, my littler brother, Joey, came into the world. My mom had always wished for a boy, so I guess that's why they tried again, and *bingo*—Joey! Joey was a little rug rat, not a Swedish blond as my sister and I are. He looks Italian! Little Joey was cute with a round face and *giant* brown puppy dog eyes. And boy was he feisty. I love having built-in friends in my siblings. We've always been very close, and to this day I call them both daily. I still wish that I hadn't had to live in Florida for twenty-five years, where I was so far away from them and where it was difficult for my kids to see their aunt and uncle regularly.

In California, my father worked as an officer with the Los Angeles Police Department. He was an integral member of the force until he retired in 1985. Prior to that, he had become an experienced airplane pilot during his tour of duty in the army and eventually got his helicopter license. Dad started the air support division within the LAPD—the first of its kind in the United States. He ended up becoming the chief pilot and trained all of the new arrivals to that division on the force. He held this position for twenty years.

We had a growing family, and his work was often dangerous. When I was twelve years old, he was flying over the airport training a colleague when something in the helicopter malfunctioned. Whether it was the helicopter or the new student he was training, they were going down! He stayed calm and focused on strategically steering away from the airplanes parked on the ground, which were full of fuel. Dad took control of the chopper as best he could, steered it to an opening, and just missed hitting two airplanes. When he crashed, he suffered a couple of bumps and bruises and some deep gashes on his legs. His student was shaken, but alive.

Being the wife of a police officer, my mom realized the dangers of my dad's job early on and let out a sigh of relief every night her husband came home safe and sound to his family. She never took his safety for granted, especially now that they had three kids.

My father was not only a man of the law at work, but he also laid down the law at home, too. I had a strict dad; he definitely kept us in line and respectful.

That was when we were young. As we got older, he could still be an intimidating force, especially when it came to dating. When guys would come to the door to pick me up for a date, he would give them the once-over and say, "Are you going to have my daughter home by eleven?" And they said, "Yes, sir." He had some kind of an air about him that the guys I dated knew not to mess with. And so did I. On *Hogan Knows Best*, when Terry shot the dating scenes with Brooke and the guys came to the front door, it reminded me of my dating years except Terry made friends with the guys. Although at times Dad seemed a bit over-protective of us kids, I realize now that he just wanted to make sure his daughters and son were safe. As a veteran police officer of twenty-five years, he had seen the ugly side of life—incidents the general public rarely hears about. My father brought home books full of crime scene photos that only police officers were allowed to see. He sat us down and made us look at photographs of murdered female hitchhikers—back in those days hitchhiking in California was the thing to do. The books had grizzly photos of victims found in the woods with decapitated heads, fingers cut off, and other atrocities. Not exactly warm and fuzzy bedtime stories for us kids. However, it surely made a point and we *never* hitchhiked.

It also gave us the kind of knowledge I think we needed for survival. It taught us how to have protective eyes, which my dad called "learning how to watch your ass." My sister and I always watched our surroundings and made sure nobody was following us. He taught us what to do if we were ever forced into a situation where we ended up in a car with a stranger. He told us to kick, scream, scratch, punch, poke—whatever we had to do to get away from that person. We hoped that we would never have to rely on this advice, but it gave my sister, brother, and me a different edge over the other kids we knew. Later on in life, if I ever argued with Terry, I think my reason for often just giving up and leaving rather than getting into it with him was a "fight or flight" mentality. Antagonizing and getting the last word in during an argument were never the answers with him. It was a lot safer to remain quiet and just disappear. My siblings and I were wise about many things thanks to our father. Being the child of a police officer was a different way of life, but it worked well for our family. All of the kids turned out with good morals and values.

My mother brought a creative vision to our family, one that I think rubbed off on me. She's an extremely gifted interior designer and over the years has helped many people around Los Angeles with their homes. She was a stay-at-home mom who dabbled in designing until I was eighteen years old and she opened up her own interior design shop in Westlake Village, California—a suburb of L.A. My mom was and still is today a prominent interior designer in the Los Angeles area. Television and movie stars often live outside of the hub of Hollywood. They have big monster homes and land in places like the Valley. Many celebrities have used my mother's services because she offers high-end upscale design.

One day, to my mother's surprise, legendary Italian actress

Sophia Loren walked into her shop. Sophia has always been a symbol of great beauty and elegance combined with a salt-of-the-earth quality. My mother went to Sophia's home to help her put the finishing touches on an old, lavish ranch house that she had owned for years. Although she was humble, a quick look around her home reflected that she was indeed Hollywood royalty. There was Sophia in framed photos with everyone from leading men like Cary Grant to world leaders like Mikhail Gorbachev. Sophia had exquisite taste in art and there were some breathtaking paintings on the walls, including some Rembrandt etchings. My mother was a bit taken by a particularly morose-looking painting that was one of the largest pieces on her walls. Because it was filled with dark colors and ugly faces, she felt it was a real downer and had to go immediately. "Sophia, why don't we take that one down and put something really colorful up on that wall?" my mom said.

"Gail, there are only two in the world and the other one is hanging in the Louvre," Sophia responded, nonchalantly.

"Wow. Okay, it's a keeper!" Mom responded and began to admire the painting.

My mom eventually furnished Sophia's home with sofas, beautiful wall coverings, and distinctive bookcases, "bibliotecas" as Sophia liked to call them. Working for Sophia still stands as one of the crowning moments of my mother's career. With her talents, she could make a person's home look warm and classy. But they needed to add a touch of their own class to pull it off. Sophia projected class through and through. In essence, she and my mother complemented each other well and were a good team. It was exciting that my mother worked with somebody who was so famous and so classy, and, to top it off, she was Italian!

Even though my mom and dad were busy with their careers, they were never MIA as parents. They were there to help us with homework, hobbies, rides to school every day or to friends' houses, and home-cooked meals. We didn't have a lot of money, but my parents still found a way to make holidays and birthdays special with tons of presents and lots of love. One year we received new bikes, only to find out twenty years later that they were used and my dad had painted them! Even today at fifty-one years old, I can call my mom and dad anytime of the day or night and they're always there for me. After all, that's what family is for.

Sundays at Grandma's

I loved our family Italian Sunday dinners. They were always feasts. Food and fun! All my cousins, aunts, and uncles!

On the weekends we would pile into our station wagon and head over to my grandma's little ranch-style house early to begin cooking. I learned a lot from watching my mom and grandma cook. Who knew I was going to marry a three-hundred-pound wrestler with the appetite of three men? Trust me, I eventually put *everything* I learned in the kitchen as a young girl to use cooking for my hubby. I had to make a lot of food and make it *fast*!

Nobody in my family was shy about eating. Grandma made sure there was always enough for everyone. And at our dinner table everything was homemade and real (except maybe Grandma's dye job). We would get fresh eggs from her chickens and tomatoes from her garden. The pasta was also made from scratch.

When it comes to Italian food, my mom has always had a motto: if you cook it, they will come. And, boy, was she right! Besides our immediate family—which was fairly large—there seemed to be a constant revolving door bringing people in and out of Grandma's house, including the priest, Father Fitzpatrick, from the local parish. Another one of my mother's celebrity clients from her interior design business was Dick Van Patten of *Eight Is Enough* fame. He heard about these traditional Sunday dinners and wanted to come join us for the festivities. Dick became a die-hard fan of my mom and grandmother's cooking. He joined us many times, bringing his wife and two sons. He had a great sense of humor and was a genuinely down-to-earth man. Wow, did they love the homemade wine and playing bocce in Grandma's front yard! It was like having a touch of Italy in the San Fernando Valley. Even Dick began to spread the good word about the good food served.

One time, when my mom was working at Dick's house, Farrah Fawcett happened to be visiting him. He started raving about my grandmother's cooking, and Farrah immediately became intrigued. She was amazed that our family did this big Sunday dinner on every weekend, without fail.

"Gail, why haven't you invited me?" Farrah asked.

Why didn't I invite Farrah Fawcett to my mother's for dinner? Mom wondered, shocked. Probably because, at the time, Farrah was the resident angel on *Charlie's Angels* and one of the most famous actresses in the world.

"Would you like to join us for dinner some Sunday?" Mom asked.

"Of course, I'd like to come over *this* coming Sunday," she responded, enthusiastically.

Mom went home and told my grandmother that on this particular Sunday we would need to make a meal fit for a queen—or an angel, that is. Mom said to her, "We're going to have a few extra people over this Sunday. In fact, a *big* star is coming over for dinner."

"How big? How many eggs do I need to put in the pasta?" answered Grandma. To Grandma, a "big" movie star meant a *large* movie star, like Clint Eastwood or John Wayne. When she made the homemade pasta, the recipe called for one egg per person.

My family considered Farrah to be Hollywood royalty. We wanted to make it a special day for her, but when she arrived at our home on that Sunday afternoon, we quickly realized that the red carpet treatment was the last thing that she wanted. Farrah didn't seem impressed with herself and was eager to learn about us when we all sat down at the dinner table. Quickly, Farrah became like one of the family, with her southern grace. The glamorous star we watched every week on national TV showed a warmth of personality that took everyone by surprise. Farrah possessed a special innocence and loved the sense of family she got from sitting around and laughing with us. It just confirmed that no matter how famous someone is, everyone needs a sense of home. My family took pride in offering that to her and others who came to our house to eat.

I'm four years older than my brother and sister, so I always helped with the dinners when we were growing up. We rarely went out to eat. We would be lucky if we got a bucket of Kentucky Fried Chicken on the weekends. Later on in life, my mother was really good about teaching my sister and me how to cook. I was always interested in learning her recipes and little tricks. I was a little overweight as a preteen and my father would sit at the other end of the table and say jokingly, "Okay, Linda, which leg are you going to put that in?" or he'd ask me how much bigger I wanted my feet to get. He could be a pretty funny guy, too! My siblings and I would laugh at dinner, sometimes making our drinks explode out of our noses!

Mom was always good about making more than enough food for everybody. She would make sure to feed the men! She told me that you always want to have something cooking when people come over because the smell of food on the stove draws them in. It made a house a home. I always did that in my marriage to Terry, whether it was coffee brewing, a cake baking, or chili simmering on the stove. It would bring people together. (Quick tip: Brown an onion!)

During all of those Sunday dinners at Grandma's every week, I didn't realize what kind of impact they would have on me later in life and how I would end up entertaining the same way as an adult. When I was a kid, my grandmother could feed an army of people, while still laughing and having fun doing it. And everybody was always welcome. Family, friends, friends of friends, neighbors—she never turned anyone away. That influence made its way into my life.

Being married to a wrestler, I found that the kitchen was the hub of our home. I was always cooking for the fellas. Even though Terry and I didn't come from money and he eventually became really famous, we had this yearning to remain grounded and welcome all kinds of guests into our home. People weren't going to a big celebrity's house; they were just going to Terry and

Linda's house. And guests knew that if they came over to our house, it would be a feast with beer and wine, kids, and tons of food. It was always a good time.

These recipes are from my mom, Aunt Rosie, Grandma Ciccarelli, and Aunt Judy. I'll always remember all the delicious Sunday dinners with my family!

Pasta Sauce

2 pounds pork bones (neck bones or farmers' ribs)
olive oil
3 cloves garlic, minced
1 gallon tomato sauce
3 tablespoons chopped parsley

Brown the neck bones in olive oil; add the garlic and cook for one minute. Add the tomato sauce and parsley. Cover and simmer for about 2 hours. Add salt and pepper to taste.

When sauce is done, you can add parmesan cheese for additional flavor.

Grandma Ciccarelli's Biscotti

Makes 2 dozen

6 eggs
2 cups sugar
½ cup vegetable oil
3 tablespoons extract (any flavor you like)
4½ cups all-purpose flour
1 tablespoon baking powder
¼ teaspoon salt
2 cups chocolate chips
1 cup dried cranberries
1½ cups chopped walnuts
powdered cocoa or cinnamon (to taste)

Preheat oven to 350 degrees. In a large bowl, beat together the eggs, sugar, oil, and extract. Once mixed together, add the flour, baking powder, and salt. Mix together. Then add the chocolate chips, cranberries, and walnuts as well as the spice (cinnamon or cocoa). Knead it together.

On two nonstick cookie sheets, form the dough into four large logs (two logs per tray). Bake 25 minutes at 350 degrees. Remove from the oven and immediately cut each log horizontally into thirds. Lift each section and place onto a cutting board. Cut each section into one-inch slices and place the individual slices back onto the cookie sheet on their sides. Put them back into the oven for 10 to 15 minutes (or until slightly brown). Take the cookie sheets out and let cool. Serve warm or at room temperature.

Valley Girls Like to Party

Growing up, I felt like a geek. I was terrible at sports. I was the typical kid who nobody picked to be on their team. I'd basically sit on the bench and eat lunch all by myself.

Although I didn't have many friends in class, I did have a few who lived on my block. Immediately after doing our homework, we'd go outside and play until dark. We'd play dress up, dodge ball, pogo stick, and Chinese jump rope. We'd ride bikes. We'd chill out in someone's tree house. Now that I look back, those are the things that kids are missing out on today—good, clean, wholesome fun.

As a kid, I had long, blond hair, and I didn't bother to take care of it. I was a tan, outdoorsy girl. I didn't wear any makeup. I went to school, did my homework, and helped my mom around the house. I loved to swim and ride my bike. I only had a couple of girlfriends and spent a lot of time babysitting my younger siblings. I didn't have much of a social life outside of my neighborhood.

As I headed into the ninth grade at Chaminade Catholic Prep School, I decided to try out for the cheerleading squad. I thought that maybe this would help jump-start my social life. Well, I didn't end up making it. I was devastated. I immediately went from an unpopular chick, to an *unpopular* chick who didn't make the cheerleading squad. Then, I learned a very important lesson: it's never over until it's over. Soon after, I got a call from the cheerleading coach saying that one of the girls on the squad was moving and I was the next in line to shake her pom-poms. Just like that, I was a junior varsity cheerleader!

Almost overnight, my whole life changed. People who never knew my name were now passing me in the hallway saying "Hi, Linda!" Pep rallies, football games, basketball games, school fund-raisers—you name it, I was cheering at it. I was always full of energy. The quarterback asked me out. In fact, I had every football player on the team looking to score a touchdown with me. Who knew that all I had to do was put on a cheerleading uniform to go from geek to chic.

I think the life lessons I learned as a cheerleader were important. Cheerleading gave me confidence. I became more outgoing. I learned how to laugh. Most important, I learned how to network with other girls instead of being jealous of them. This has served me well in life. Like the old saying, "Keep your friends close and your enemies closer."

Just when my social life seemed to be on cruise control, my parents pulled the emergency brake. By the end of eleventh grade, tuition went up at my private school, and my mom informed me that they couldn't afford it any longer. I would now have to attend a public school. *What?!* I thought, stunned. *Right before my senior year?* It took me so many years to fit into a school with seven hundred kids. Now I had to start all over again in a public school with twenty-five hundred . . . whoa!

My first day of public school in the Valley was shocking! I walked into the bathroom of Chatsworth High before class and girls were smoking cigarettes. I even smelled pot. This was a far cry from what I had been exposed to at my prior rules-oriented Catholic school. But I soon thought this school was a cakewalk compared to Catholic school. It was like one big party! You could dress and wear your hair just like you wanted. I didn't have to wear a school uniform, and I decided that this was going to be a blast! I welcomed the change of wearing bright colors, short skirts, and platform shoes. Wanana! Surfers rule!

In one of my classes, I met a girl named Gina who would quickly become my running mate. Gina and I were like two peas in a pod . . . or, rather, two Valley girls in the valley. We were like clones. We both had long blond hair and green eyes, we were the same exact height, and we dressed alike. We loved to listen to the same music. We even spoke the same: "Like, oh my God, gag me with a spoon!" (Yeah, Valley girls actually said stuff like that.) We also both liked cutting class and watching the cute surfers in Malibu instead of going to fourth period. It didn't take long for me to forget all the rules!

On the weekends during high school, we'd go out at night to twenty-one and older dance clubs. Gina had a fake ID, and I scored one, too. Mine was from my friend's sister who didn't look anything like me, and her name was Leslie. One night, I walked into a club and when the bouncer looked at my ID, I think he knew it wasn't me in the photo. "Leslie, do you mind signing our guest book?" he asked.

"Sure," I said. Then, I signed it as Linda.

"Okay, *Linda*," he said looking down at the book. "I thought your name was Leslie?"

"Ah . . . yeah, well, sometimes people call me Linda and other times Leslie," I responded nervously, trying to win him over with my Pepsodent smile.

"By the way," the bouncer said, "I really love the name necklace you're wearing that says 'Linda' on it."

Busted! I totally forgot about my necklace. That was really stupid.

Back then, I was certainly developing into a young woman. I grew up with a beautiful mother, which made an impression on me and my style forever. When my mom would go out with my dad, she would get dressed up just like a movie star. She looked hot! If you thought the '80s had big hair, the '60s had even bigger hair. And my mom was the queen of the big hair! I learned a lot by watching my mother get ready. She would put on black eyeliner to create cat eyes. Then, she'd apply some fiery red lipstick and put on a cute little dress. Look out! To this day I try to make an impact with my style as well.

I never had naturally big breasts growing up (at that time I was just a size B). Having babies and nursing them changed everything. After I was done breast-feeding Brooke, my boobs looked like two zucchinis! And, as if you couldn't tell, I had my boobs done. It was the age of Pamela Anderson, and big boobs were a huge fad. Then, after breast-feeding Nick, I decided to have them done again for the same reason. Eventually, the scar tissue in one of my implants got hard, so I needed to do them yet again. You see, girls, you never know what you're in for! My mother tells me to get them reduced, but I never heard a guy complain that they were too big. So I'm leaving them as is. (Quick tip: Don't fix it if it's not broken!)

I realized at Chatsworth that I actually had a pretty good set of legs on me, probably from cheerleading at Chaminade for three years. You would have never noticed my legs under the plaid skirt of the Catholic school uniform. Going to Chatsworth

High and showing off my muscular tan legs with the miniskirts with the cute shoes was really fun. I was digging it and noticed it was getting the attention of the boys.

A tall, handsome PE coach who worked at my brother and sister's school definitely caught my eye. He had nice legs, bulging biceps, long, brown surfer hair, and a thick mustache. Actually, come to think of it, he looked more like a '70s porn star than a PE teacher. But I know what I like!

When I would pick up my brother and sister at school, he would usually greet me by coming over to my car window. We chatted for a bit and pretty soon he asked me out on a date. Sure he was a bit older, but he was really hot! We went out a few times and eventually we went back to his apartment. After he did some convincing, we ended up in bed. Was the sex good or bad? I had no clue. Was his big or small? I had no idea. I was a virgin. When it was all said and done and he rolled off me, I noticed that something was missing.

"Where's the condom?" I asked, looking down at his uncovered member.

"I don't know," he replied, confused.

"What do you mean, 'you don't know'?! *You* were the one wearing it!"

I began freaking out. Even though it was my first time having sex, I didn't think a condom could just fly off! Or could it? I jumped up and frantically searched the bed, the floor, and under the bed. There was no condom in sight. Then, it hit me. "Oh my God. Maybe it's in here," I said, pulling it out from you know where.

I'm screwed, I thought. *Just my luck, the first time I go and have sex I'll probably get pregnant.*

I sweated bullets every day for the next three weeks until my period came. Phew! I quickly realized that no sexual protection is foolproof. Eventually, I got over the condom crisis, and between the surfers in Malibu, the hot guys on the dance floor, and the PE teacher I still saw every now and then, my life had definitely changed.

TWO BLONDES
WALK INTO A BAR . . .

*G*RADUATION DAY CAME. FINALLY! I HAD HAD SENIORI-
tis since the eleventh grade, and now it was finally
over. My girlfriend Gina and I sat in the bleachers wearing
powder-blue caps and gowns waiting for our names to be called.
When we got our scrolls, Gina's was signed, but mine had a note
to see the principal about summer school.

I had failed a government course miserably and that prevented
me from getting a diploma. Learning about how the House of
Representatives and the Senate function seemed überboring to
me. Hitting the beach with my girlfriends seemed so much more
productive.

While my friends headed off to the beach first thing in the morning, I headed to summer school. From Monday through Friday for two months straight, I sat in a portable classroom trailer with a broken air conditioner studying our government. It's a wonder that I ever voted after that!

Even though I hadn't graduated from high school at that point, I did graduate from beauty school and set my sights in that direction. I eventually made it through summer school, took my final exams, and finally passed government. It was clear that college wasn't going to be my thing and I was fine with that. Surprisingly, my mom and dad were fine with it, too. I think they believed that I would be successful in any way that I applied myself. I was a chip off the old block. I had my dad's work ethic and logic and my mother's creativity. I was a ball of fire and a people person who always spoke my mind. I never sat back. As a kid I always wanted to know why and couldn't easily be pacified. Even though I was a geek in grade school, I still had a mind of my own and marched to the beat of my own drum. Also, being around girls cheerleading made me realize that I actually had a personality and I was funny. People liked to hang around me and I had friends who liked me for me, and this was shocking because I had so few friends early on.

One of my mother's friends owned a nail shop and my mom got a tip (no pun intended) that there was an opening for a job. I went to the salon and was interviewed. They must have liked me because I was hired to start immediately.

The nail shop was a cool place to work. Our salon was filled with cute Valley girls doing nails in bright, funky colors. I think the customers enjoyed it and kept coming back. The salon was located in an upper-middle-class area of the Valley. In an economy where many women couldn't afford the luxury of a manicure, these more affluent women could. I had a lot of Jewish clients, too, and one Hanukkah they all got together and bought me a gold chai symbol, which in Hebrew means "life." They said that they were all adopting me and they were now my Jewish mothers. *Love you guys*, I thought. *But one mother's advice is enough!*

In just a couple of months, I ended up building a solid clientele at the salon and was banking about $450 a week, which was really good money back in the late '70s. I gave up my red VW Bug and bought a brand-new black 1978 Camaro. I got an apartment. Quickly, I was on my own and rolling.

I realized that being a manicurist is almost like being a bartender. As I buffed, filed, and painted, I would sit and listen to every one of my clients' problems, family stories, and love lives just like a bartender listens to a customer on a stool with a beer in hand. I was like a shrink with a new client every hour on the hour with a new story! Family problems, cheating husbands, bratty kids, bitchy girlfriends, interfering in-laws—the topics ran the gamut from A to Z. One thing I learned from all of my single female customers was that you should never live with somebody unless you're married to them, because some guys thought, Why buy the cow when you can get the milk for free? So many of my female clients moved in with their boyfriends and just three months later they were packing up their stuff and moving out. Another thing I realized from my career as a manicurist was that there is always a new life lesson to be learned from someone else's mistakes.

I was happy with the money, but things were beginning to get difficult. There was gossip about clients as they walked out the door, and I don't dig gossip!

The owner of the shop had a chance to be a contestant on the game show *Match Game* and won a trip to Acapulco. "If you guys want to be a contestant, I can get you on the show," she told us. Although I had never watched *Match Game* on television, a free vacation sounded pretty darn good to me. So one afternoon a few of us girls from the salon went to the CBS Television Studios and tried out. After a series of interviews, the producers ended up picking me as a contestant. *Acapulco, here I come!* I thought.

The host of *Match Game*, Gene Rayburn, coordinated all the action while the six-celebrity panel was given a phrase with one word missing. The celebs would write down the word that they believed was the best possibility to help make the match. Then, two contestants would try to guess what the stars had chosen. The key to the game was to pick the most basic thing. A point was given for each correct match, and the contestant with the most points won.

The bright lights, cameras, audience, and excitement—I was a Valley girl who was simple at heart and was a bit intimidated when I stepped out onto the set. However, I quickly composed myself and got down to business. I made some matches and was doing pretty well. In the end, I actually had the most points for the day.

In the final round I went head-to-head with one celebrity— the comedian and Broadway actor Charles Nelson Reilly, who was a frequent panelist on the program. I had the chance to win $5,000. The final match question was: Princess BLANK. The first thing I could think of was Princess Grace, so I blurted it out. Then, Rayburn asked Reilly what he chose and he said, "Princess Grace." *Ding, ding, ding!* I won $5,000! I was jumping up and down. I ended up going home with a total of $5,500.

In the summer of 1978, I opened Linda's Nail Boutique in Chatsworth, California. Having been exposed to my mom's interior design ideas and talents, I knew I wanted to do something different decorwise in my new place. First I bought a bunch of old antique treadle sewing machines; then I took the machines out of the table stands and used the table frames as workstations. They were very unusual and caught the eye of every customer as soon as they walked into my shop. I designed the shop with an all-Victorian motif, including an antique dresser with a big mirror over it, potted parlor palms, and cute floral wallpaper, all in the beautiful colors of lavender and soft greens. It was very feminine. I hired a new crew and even had a guy manicurist, which was pretty much unheard of then.

Linda's Nail Boutique quickly became known as one of the hippest manicure salons in the Valley. I knew that with busy careers and even busier family lives with screaming kids and demanding husbands, many of the housewives in my area were in need of a little TLC, and I knew exactly how to deliver it. As soon as they walked in, clients heard relaxing jazz music. Complimentary coffee was served in the morning, and white wine was available after three P.M. I offered all the latest fashion magazines and even threw *Playgirl* into the mix, which was new on the horizon back in those days. Let me tell you, the women you wouldn't think would have ever picked up a *Playgirl* always picked it up. When they turned the magazine sideways and the centerfold—"man of the month"—would unfold, I'd always let out a little chuckle. In fact, we had a damn good time in there. It was like a party. Many of the customers also became my friends, and I still keep in contact with them today. I worked long hours and always did my best. I made it a fun place to be. The customers really liked my caring style.

Linda's Nail Boutique was a success. Blonde ambition, baby!

The Game of Dating

All work and no play takes the fun out of Linda's day, I thought. I wasn't even twenty-one years old yet and I was busier than most adults I knew. I owned my own flourishing business and condo, which I bought with the money I was making at the salon. However, even though I was crazy busy, I was young and needed to keep up my social life. I decided to play my hand at the game of dating. One day, the most gorgeous set of long, tan, muscular legs walked into my nail salon. I looked up and saw it was the new mailman on our route. *Talk about a special delivery,* I thought. *Wow, nice* package*!*

The mailman's name was Steve. He had dark curly hair and wore aviator sunglasses and shorts. When he entered my store, he appeared nervous because of all the girls checking him out. I decided to break the ice and introduce myself. As we talked and I looked into his hazel eyes, I began wishing mail was delivered on Sundays, too. I decided to invite Steve to my mother's house for a barbecue.

Eventually we began dating exclusively. It was a simple relationship, but really fun. We'd go to the movies and then to Bob's Big Boy for a burger and a milk shake. Steve bought an old red Corvette and we would go on long drives along the coast on weekends. I really enjoyed spending time with him and we had a lot of laughs.

My mom wasn't afraid to offer her opinions on the men I dated. "You could have a jet-set life if you wanted. You need to take a moment to think about all the options you have."

I was young and didn't know that I was worthy of a jet-set life. Steve was my first real boyfriend, and all I knew in my youthful naïveté was that even though he didn't have a lot of money, I just enjoyed being with him. I was simple at heart just like he was. I was not the gold-digging type.

Toward the end, my relationship with Steve unfortunately began to unravel from the confusion of my heart and my head not really aligning. I wondered if maybe I did need to explore life a bit more. After three years of dating, we broke up and I really missed him. I guess my mom just wanted the best for me. She always used to tell me that I was beautiful, special, and a ball of fire. She felt I needed to date guys who had more to offer than just good looks, nice legs, and a sweet disposition.

After I broke up with Steve, I decided to play the field for a little bit. We had become serious, and I needed to see where my own life was heading. I was a little older now, and I wanted to date different types of guys. I didn't care if they were geeks or cool, older or younger. For the next year, I opened my mind up and expanded my dating horizons. Along with the dating I was doing, my mom decided to do a little guy hunting on her own for me.

A client of my mother's design firm, Claridge House Interiors, had four kids, and one of their sons was a big, strong twenty-three-year-old contractor who looked a lot like the actor Tom Selleck. Well, that piqued my interest for sure, so I decided to do my own investigation on the *Magnum P.I.* look-alike. I found out that Brad was six foot four, with brown hair and green eyes. He was heavily involved in his Christian church, kind of like a born-again Christian.

After going to Catholic school for eleven years and attending mass every Sunday, I was kind of burned out on spending my Sundays at the parish hall. Not that I was tired of being Catholic; it's just that I was working like a fiend and my weekends were precious. Getting dressed in my Sunday best and sitting in a hot church was not how I wanted to spend my weekends. I wanted to get dressed in my best bikini and head to the beach.

My mom didn't think that being a born-again Christian was so bad. "It wouldn't hurt you to go to church more often," she said. *Maybe she's right,* I thought. *How bad could this be?* After all, I was dating all kinds. So one Sunday afternoon Brad and I met for our first date at—where else?—his church.

Brad and I clicked and dated for about a year. Although we spent Sundays at church, we did eventually make it to the beach together, just not the way I had expected. He invited me on Valentine's Day and wanted to make sure we were sitting on the sand at sunset, which I thought was really sweet. As we both watched the sun sink behind the sea, Brad seemed supernervous, and I began to get a sinking feeling. He rambled on and on about how much he loved me. Brad also looked increasingly pale, and when he held my hand, his palm was clammier than the oysters we had earlier for lunch.

"Is everything okay?" I asked.

Then he hit me with it. "Linda, will you marry me?" he said, as he popped the question.

Marriage? I thought. It had only been a year. I was totally shocked. I wasn't ready for that serious a step, but clearly Brad was.

He looked at me with fear in his eyes and said, "Linda, answer me. Will you marry me?"

"Ah . . . sure, yes. Yes, I'll marry you."

Brad went home and told his entire family about the engagement and that I said yes. It was clearly such a big deal in his family. He was his parents' favorite. The happier and more excited they got, the more scared I got.

As time went by, I realized in my heart of hearts that I wasn't going to marry Brad. And as more time passed, the pressure mounted. From selecting a wedding location to creating a guest list to booking a honeymoon suite, the wedding train was quickly leaving the station and I felt like lying down on the tracks.

I continued to go through the motions for the next couple of months, but as each day passed I realized how different Brad and I were. When it was time to pick out the bridesmaids' dresses, I began to get really nervous. I had to speak up and say something. I drove to my mom's house, sobbing the entire way. I had to speak my mind. I needed her help to get out of this thing.

I sat my mother down and told her the truth. She helped me call off the wedding. My mother and I both learned a valuable lesson that day. There's no way in the world that any daughter can marry the person a parent selects for her, despite all the good intentions involved. Just because Brad was a good, clean Christian man doesn't mean he was the right marriage material for me.

I think my mother realized that I, the extrovert and wild child I was, had to alter myself too much to be with a person like Brad. I think she understood the importance of me staying true to myself and she helped me get out of it by calling his mom and breaking the ice. I was so scared!

I had a friendly, fun-loving spirit. Adventurous. And guys really dug it. Unfortunately, it got me into situations that led to serious relationships way too quickly. The guy starts calling me every day. We start seeing each other every day. Next thing you know we're going steady! After breaking it off with Brad, I decided to stay single for one of the first times in my life. In trying to be serious with my love life, I came up with the policy "three strikes and you're out." (Strike 1: His conversation over dinner is duller than the butter knife. Strike 2: He picks his teeth after dinner and eats it. Yuck! Strike 3: You are out with a guy and he leaves a crappy tip . . . you're like, huh?) Dealing with one or two of these things you think to yourself, *Maybe I can deal with this*. But when strike 3 hits, he's out.

After a few dates like that, I decided that being single wasn't so bad. You start to realize that your time is more valuable. You'd rather sit home and read a good book than be out with some chump, having to fake it all night. I decided that I didn't want to waste my time anymore.

In 1981, I ended up meeting a woman named Cindy, who worked at the nail salon. Some of the manicurists I worked with were housewives and others young unmarried girls, but most everybody in there was average. Cindy dared to be different. We called her Crazy Cindy! She had platinum blond hair, wore fake eyelashes every day, was always tan, and had a great set of legs. She was thirty-six years old, divorced with four kids, but she had the energy of a teenager. She was a big influence on me because she made everything look like fun and was a great mom! We hung out constantly, going to the beach, working out, and even dieting together.

This was the time when I started to really come into my own, getting into shape and figuring out my own style. The '80s workout craze was starting to take over, and I was into going to the gym—the social scene there was great. Tanning beds were becoming popular, too, and I would get bronze by visiting the tanning salon three times a week. I loved to dress in neon colors, because it described how happy I was inside at that time. I would wear long dragon lady nails in sunset red or coral. My body was curvaceous and muscular. I had lost ten pounds, and I was enjoying feeling so confident and self-assured.

I was meeting new people and just as I was starting to feel good about myself . . . BAM! I met Terry—the one man who would make me *wrestle* with my decision to *stay* single.

Locking Lips with Thunderlips

I was twenty-two and I had owned my nail shop for four years and a condo that I bought for $76,000. Every month I had a mortgage payment, nail shop rent, utilities, and a car payment, and I got tired of struggling so hard to make ends meet. I took a second job and began cocktail waitressing at one of the Mexican restaurants that a client of my nail shop owned. I then worked at a French bistro hoping I could make more money. I would get up at seven A.M to work at the nail shop, change clothes in the bathroom at the end of the day, and then work at the bar till two thirty A.M. Then, I would go to sleep and do the same thing the next day. I couldn't keep going at this pace, and it was too much stress for a girl in her early twenties.

In the summer of 1982, I sold the shop, rented out my condo, and moved back home with my parents. Then, I started working at my friend's nail salon. I knew the transition to moving back in with Mom and Dad wasn't going to be easy, but my bigger goal was to save money. Almost immediately after I moved home, I bought a brand-new red Corvette. This really pissed off my mom.

"I thought you moved back home to *save* money?" my mom griped.

"I *am* going to save. I promise!" I said with conviction, as if I had to convince myself.

One Friday night, I had to work late at the nail salon. I hadn't made plans with any of my girlfriends for after work. I really needed to get out, but everyone already had plans. Feeling sort of sorry for me, my mom suggested we go to the movies to see *E.T.* I thought, *A Martian movie?* (Little did I know that cute alien would phone home into the hearts of people everywhere.) Reluctantly, I got into my family's station wagon, and my mom and I went to the Winnecka 4 Drive-In Movie Theater. I felt like a total loser at twenty-two years old going to the movies with my mommy on a Friday night! But she really helped me get out of the doldrums.

When we got to the theater, *E.T.* was sold out. My mom suggested we see *Rocky III*, which was the other popular movie playing.

"I don't want to see a boxing movie," I said. "I hate boxing."

"No, it's a love story. You'll like it!" my mom said, enthusiastically.

Shortly after the plot of the film unfolded, there was a scene where this big, tan, muscular blond guy called Thunderlips came on-screen. He was slated to fight Rocky in a charity match. Thunderlips had a presence that could not be ignored. As he flexed his pecs with four beautiful blondes climbing all over him, he looked at Rocky and said arrogantly, "The ultimate man versus the ultimate meatball." It was a part of the movie that you really remembered.

The next morning as soon as I woke up, I called my friend Kathy, who was another manicurist. "I *had to* go to the drive-in with my mom last night," I said, and then I continued, "so we're going dancing tonight and I don't care if I have to drag you out!"

That night, Kathy and I hit the town. We headed over to the nightclub Red Onion, on Canoga Avenue in Woodland Hills. It was a popular spot for local Valley girls, with a disco downstairs. We had only been there five minutes when Kathy said, "Hey, the guy from the *Rocky* movie is here tonight."

"Sylvester Stallone?" I asked.

"No, the other guy."

"Clubber Lang?"

"No, the big blond guy."

My heart pounded because Kathy was absolutely right! With his long blond hair, Thunderlips, wearing tinted sunglasses, stood towering—and I mean *towering*—over the sea of club-goers. As he made his way into the club, I noticed him talking to a few groupies. *I am* not *going to be one of them*, I said to myself, and kept my distance.

I couldn't help but think about the fate in all of this. I never go to the movies, and then the one movie *I do* go to see, the very next night the guy from the movie is right in front of me. In my town. In my club! It was so darn crazy that he was there. One night before, I wouldn't have known him from Adam!

While I was on the dance floor, his friend Nelson asked me to dance. I think it made Thunderlips kind of jealous because he kept staring and eventually came over. He said in a low voice, "Hey, excuse me. Can I buy you a drink?"

"Sure," I said, nonchalantly. Then I turned to Kathy and whispered excitedly, "He wants to buy me a drink."

Thunderlips came back with the drinks and introduced himself as Hulk Hogan. "Uh, what? Hunk what?" I said, not sure if I heard him correctly. We danced a bit and drank some more. Later, we stood in front of the cigarette machine where it was quieter and talked. For a massive guy, he had a gentleness about him. Hulk told me he was a professional wrestler. *Wrestling?* I thought. Back in those days, there was no wrestling on television on the West Coast like the kind of entertainment the WWE offers today. It was just Mexican wrestlers in masks who didn't speak English, seen on local Spanish stations at three A.M. I really didn't know what he meant. I thought Hulk was an actor. "Is wrestling like boxing?" I asked.

As we spoke, Hulk rubbed his body against mine. He was so big and tall and had incredible presence. I remember his jeans being really tight, and he was so tall that his package was up to my chest.

At the end of the night, when Kathy and I were getting into my Corvette at the valet's desk, Hulk suddenly pulled up, sitting in the passenger seat of his friend's beater. He asked me for my phone number. I'm not sure if I was playing hard to get or just plain scared because he was so big, but I didn't give him my number. Then he asked me where I worked.

"I work at Chatsworth Nail Designs," I said.

"What's the number?" Hulk asked.

"It's in the phone book," I yelled, as we drove off. Earlier in the evening he had mentioned that he lived in Minnesota, and I figured that I would never see him again, so what was the point.

The next day, when I arrived at work, I told the girls at the salon all about meeting Thunderlips. I answered a flurry of questions: *What was he like? Was he as big in person? Is his hair really that blond?* They thought our chance meeting was really cool, and all the ladies were on high alert in case he called. But I really didn't think he heard me outside the club; even if he did, I didn't think he'd hunt the number down. Later that day the receptionist came up to me and said, "Hulk Hogan is on the phone."

Oh my God, really? I can't believe he found my number! I never thought he'd really call.

My heart immediately raced as I answered. His voice was low

and sexy. I was so nervous! He told me that he wanted to hook up again since he was visiting for a few more days. We ended up meeting at the same bar because he didn't know his way around. His friend dropped him off, and later I realized that I had to give him a ride home. We were at the bar for a total of five minutes when he asked me if I wanted to get out of there.

"Where do you want to go?" I asked.

"Do you mind if we go for a drive?" he responded.

We got into my Corvette and I let him drive. It just seemed right. Hulk and I headed south along Freeway 101 with the wind blowing through our equally long golden blond hair. Freaky enough, the *Rocky* theme song "Eye of the Tiger" started playing on the radio! *Wow*, I thought. *Ironic to the tenth power. Rocky music playing. Thunderlips behind the wheel.* My head was spinning. About ten minutes later, we got off at the Coldwater Canyon exit because he wanted to stop by his agent's to pick something up.

After we went upstairs in an old noisy elevator, we entered his agent's dingy-ass apartment. Hulk's rep was asleep face-first on his bed in his room with the door open (clearly not the image of a power player in Hollywood). *Ooo-kay*, I thought. Hulk closed the door and took me into the other bedroom where he was staying.

"Do you want a drink?" Hulk asked me, quietly. We both had a beer. I was sitting on the edge of the bed and he said he'd be right back. Hulk disappeared into the bathroom.

He was in there for what seemed like forever, as I waited. I just felt uncomfortable since this definitely wasn't my normal type of date. It was at that moment that I snapped back to reality. *What am I doing here?* I thought. *I live at home now and it's really late. My dad's a cop. My mom is probably waiting up for me. And I don't even know this guy!*

Just as I was thinking of walking out of the apartment, Hulk nonchalantly walked out of the bathroom, *completely naked!*

There was a long silence as I gazed at Hulk's overwhelming body. What I originally thought was fat in his jeans was clearly muscle on top of muscle on top of muscle. I had never seen anyone so massive. What was he thinking? Did he think I'd be that easy?

As I sat on the edge of the bed, I questioned my normally good judgment. At first I wanted to get up and run out of the apartment, thinking *What am I doing?!* But he convinced me to stay. This was so wrong, but I stayed anyway.

I locked up with Thunderlips. He's a Leo—the king of the jungle. Man meets woman. Man wants woman. It was almost primal. We were both young. Both hot for each other. I remember him crawling on top of me and starting to kiss me. He was six foot seven. I was touching muscles so big I became submissive and just let him take me over. He was so sexy and strong. He started going for it and the next thing I knew my legs were up over my head, the pillow was folding up around my face with his massive chest right above me. The sex was probably great, but I was too worried about trying to find my next breath!

It was exciting, but I just felt so guilty. I felt bad because I thought that he probably had girls everywhere and that he'd never call me back. He'd go home to Minnesota and forget about me. I had been in such great control of myself about the guys I was going out with. I had gone three months without having sex with anyone and here I felt like a slut! I liked sex with guys, but I had to go out with them for more than one night before we went to bed. But on the way home, I realized that it was a great time. And it would definitely make for great conversation at the nail shop the next day. *An exciting one-night stand and worth it, I thought to myself. And besides, how many people can say they fucked a giant?*

Chapter Three

RINGSIDE

OR THE NEXT FEW WEEKS, ALL THE GIRLS AT WORK would whisper and giggle and say, "Oooh, Linda, it's Hulk calling again!" And Terry called me a lot! I thought this might not be a fling, but a thing. Through the conversations that we had on the phone at work or at home at night I learned more about Terry. I would ask him stuff about his background and how he got into wrestling. Even though he tried to explain what he did, it was hard to wrap my head around it.

I had no idea who Terry *really* was. In fact, I didn't even understand what he did for a living. *Who is he?* I wondered. *Is he Terry Bollea? Is he Hulk Hogan? Is he a movie star playing a wrestler? What is a wrestler?* I had so many questions. It didn't help matters that the inner workings of professional wrestling were kept top secret from the public. I knew wrestling as a sport, but I didn't know it as "sports entertainment." If Terry and I were to date seriously, I needed to know what my boyfriend actually did for a living. One day, I asked him point-blank, "What is wrestling?"

After a long pause, he responded, "You have to experience it to comprehend it."

He sent me fifty magazines in the mail so I could see exactly who he was and what he did. I didn't know much about the wrestling moves or the guys in the magazines. I only knew that whoever Terry was, he was famous. He graced every cover and centerfold, but most of the magazines were in Japanese. No one in America really knew about wrestling and Hulk Hogan yet, but Terry was a huge star in Japan.

A week later, Terry flew me to one of his matches in Denver, Colorado. I landed a few hours before the event began and met up with Terry. We had lunch, went up to our hotel room, and got in a prematch workout in the form of wild sex.

This was only the second time I had physically ever seen or been with him. But we picked up right where we had left off. Sex was intense. He was aggressive and wasn't afraid to take what he wanted. Shortly after sex, we both got up and looked at each other as we noticed some odd black gook all over the sheets. *Oh my God*, I thought. Not really knowing each other all that well yet, I began to suspect the worst.

Terry looked at me and asked, "Are you having your period?"

"No, I'm not," I responded.

"What is this?" he asked, as we both backed away from the bed. At that moment we were both thinking: *Did you shit your-*

self? We didn't even have to ask each other anything; it was as if we read each other's minds.

"No. Did you?" I shot back, certain the substance was coming from *him*.

"No!" he exclaimed, certain the substance was coming from *me*.

"Well, what is it then? Are you bleeding?"

"No, are you?"

Terry got serious and "Hulked up" just like he is known to do in the ring. He bravely went over to the bed and stared down at the unknown dark substance as if it was his next opponent. He bent down, wiped his finger in it, and proceeded to smell it.

"Ew! What is it?" I shouted out, disgusted.

"It's chocolate," he said, surprised. We both let out a huge laugh. It dawned on me that as we were wrestling around, some Junior Mints that I had bought at the airport spilled out onto the bed. The body heat from us having sex melted the chocolate all over the sheets. Hence, the mystery of the black gook was solved. *Phew!*

That night, Terry—I mean Hulk Hogan—wrestled Nick Bockwinkel, who at the time was the American Wrestling Association heavyweight champion. The arena was a smoke-filled, dingy place with maybe a total of three hundred fans in attendance. It was a far cry from the "Wrestlemania craze" that would eventually take the world by storm years later.

During the match, Terry fell out of the ring onto the concrete floor. It looked as if he bumped his head pretty badly. When Terry got up and went back in the ring to lock up with Bockwinkel again, his face was covered in blood. It was a gory mess! I immediately panicked. "Is anyone going to call an ambulance?"

I yelled out from the first row. *An ambulance?* I don't think so. Nobody was even thinking about helping Hulk. In truth, the fans turned into rabid animals at the sight of his blood. They now were yelling, "More! More! We want more!" They absolutely loved it. The more violence and blood, the more crazed the audience became. I was really concerned. So much blood! And I was shocked that nobody was doing anything. But it was par for the course.

Welcome to professional wrestling.

Following the match, Terry and I went back to his hotel room. We ordered room service and I nursed his wounds by putting ice on his head. His wrestling boots and white laces were stained red with blood and he asked me to take them to the tub and wash them off. I agreed to help him, but I saw them and thought *Yuck!* I don't even know this guy and I am already acting like wifey-poo. What I didn't realize was that he gashed *himself* with a razor blade during the match to make it seem like he had been injured. And now he was actually acting like he had a huge concussion, when in truth he was really letting me dote on him and he loved the attention. When I came out of the bathroom with Terry's boots and laces looking good as new, I saw he had already fallen asleep on the bed.

The warrior needed his rest after a night of battle.

The following morning we got in a cab together and headed to the airport. For the next year, this would be a familiar scene— Terry and I parting ways at the terminal as he headed off to another city for another match and I headed back home to Los Angeles to work at the salon. We've all heard of *Sex and the City*. Well, our relationship for the next year was "sex in the city". . . and we did it in almost every one along the western seaboard.

Las Vegas, Reno, San Francisco, San Diego—you name it, we partied in it.

When Terry would come to Los Angeles to wrestle, it was always fun to have him in my hometown. We both loved the beach and bright California sunshine. I would tell my mother that Terry was visiting from out of town and I'd take off work for the duration of his stay. We'd usually spend all of Friday, Saturday, and Sunday together.

I'd pick Terry up at the airport in my Corvette and we'd go directly to the Sheraton Hotel at the corner of Ocean Avenue and Wilshire Boulevard in Santa Monica, where a room with an ocean view awaited us. It was a passionate relationship, and we always had sex first thing out of the gate. Sex in the morning, sex in the afternoon, and sex at night—with Terry everything was full throttle. Same with his diet! When you're dating a guy who is three hundred twenty-five pounds, food is a *must*. And the amount of food was like nothing I had ever seen before in my life. He and I would go down to the coffee shop in the hotel in the morning and start the food chain rolling. Terry would begin with a bowl of Raisin Bran with skim milk. Then, he'd consume twelve eggs, a grilled hamburger patty, hash browns, and wheat toast with no butter. Lunch and dinner were just as hard core.

After we finished eating, we'd put on our workout clothes and train at the world-famous Gold's Gym in Venice Beach. Working out and showing off big muscles was a popular thing back in the '80s. And Terry was one of the poster boys in that movement. The people who trained at Gold's were the kind of workout diehards who had a hundred pounds of muscle on their body.

I usually followed Terry around during his workouts. Little by little I learned more about how to get in shape. As I took more interest in working out, Terry put me on a special diet and showed me how to watch grams of fats and carbs. Pretty soon, with all the working out, healthy food, and lots of sex, I started to look pretty good. Terry and I did activities together that I had never really done with guys on dates before. It was an exciting learning experience when I spent time with him.

When Terry would leave town to headline another wrestling event card in a different city, I had my own wrestling match to contend with at home. My relationship with Terry didn't seem to work for my parents. They'd grill me with questions like, "What does he really do?" And "How can he make that kind of money from wrestling?" Truthfully, I didn't really know, but I began to think that my parents had a point.

Because of all of my traveling and hotel rendezvous, my mother accused me of being a call girl. My parents were suspicious of Terry's credibility. But he was addictive. He wasn't like anybody I had ever met before. I really enjoyed traveling and dating an exciting guy. Living life on the edge was cool, and I wasn't going to give it up no matter what my parents said.

A White Christmas

Our long-distance relationship remained hot and heavy while Terry lived in cold and snowy Minnesota wrestling for the AWA. When Christmas approached, he wanted me to spend the holiday with him. Terry had to wrestle Christmas night and suggested I come visit him and attend the match in Minnesota. Spending a major holiday together seemed like a solid step forward in our relationship. While I felt bad leaving my family on Christmas,

I knew I would just stay home bored in California watching my younger brother and sister open all of their presents. Given my feelings for Terry, I decided I'd much rather spend Christmas kissing him under the mistletoe (with a step stool, of course). I asked my parents if they would mind me leaving town and they were okay with it. So it was over the river and through the woods to the Hulkster's house I'd go!

On my way to the Los Angeles airport on Christmas morning, a creepy guy in a crappy car followed my Corvette. He looked like some kind of nut (certainly not the kind that roast on an open fire on Christmas). So I circled around and tried to lose him. Eventually, I found a parking spot and headed to my gate. The strange guy reappeared as I was walking from my car to my departure terminal. He made an obscene gesture with his tongue and his fingers. I flipped him the bird and felt kind of bad because, after all, it was Christmas morning. He got the message though and took off after that. Or so I thought. It turned out that while I was flying en route to Minnesota, this deranged man went back to my Corvette, broke into my car, and stole my registration from my glove compartment. He then proceeded to phone my parents and tell them that I had been in an accident and drugs had been confiscated from my vehicle.

When I landed at the airport in Minnesota, I heard my name being called out on the loudspeaker requesting that I report to the security office. My mother was on the phone, completely panicked because of the man who was stalking me at LAX. I assured her everything was fine and not to worry. Once my mother found out I was safe, her feelings turned to anger. She told me that I shouldn't have left the house dressed so provocatively because it was bound to encourage the wrong kind of attention. I told her it wasn't my fault, but she continued scolding me like I was ten years old. She demanded that I fly back home immediately.

When Terry picked me up at the airport, I told him what had happened and that I didn't want to go home right away. He suggested that I stay with him as planned until the problem back home blew over. He pointed out that it didn't matter if I went back today or tomorrow because the only thing that was awaiting me in California was a further nagging session by my parents. Terry was right, and I decided to stay.

Terry and I went to his apartment, got cleaned up, and prepared to head to his wrestling match. He took me into the kitchen. Then he reached above the stove, grabbed a mirror, and laid out a few lines of coke on it.

I had never done it before, and it frightened me at first. I never dreamed it was going to be *that* kind of white Christmas.

DRUGS WERE VERY PREVALENT IN THE '80S. ADD WRESTLING TO the picture, and they became a given. Those guys couldn't function without them. I actually didn't realize how prevalent drug use was in the wrestling world until Terry and I had been married a few years and I had spent time on the road with him. From life on the road to the physical brutality of the business, to the schedule and traveling, not to mention being bored and lonely on the road—it seemed like wrestlers had a reason to do every kind of drug and narcotic that was around. It also helped numb them from the pain of being injured. They were up at an ungodly hour and stayed up for an equally ungodly number of hours. The only way they could keep up with the schedule was chemically.

I understood what they were taking was prescribed for them. It seemed the only thing was that they used the drugs more heavily than what was probably directed on the prescription.

At the time, Terry and I took our relationship minute by minute. There was no talk about goals or dreams. There was no conversation about marriage or kids. We were living on the edge. It was fresh, exciting, and fun. Everything was totally different going out with Terry. Going to the gym with him was new for me. Going to wrestling matches was new for me. Hanging out with wrestlers was new for me. A date with him wasn't the typical night of going to dinner and a movie. He'd call me and ask me to fly to see him and I'd usually go. Little by little he was teaching me about the wrestling business. I also noticed that he was a king among men. He was the lead dude among all the other wrestlers. Maybe the *Rocky* movie put him there. I don't know. But I just saw that he had a presence that none of the other wrestlers had. I usually got bored with guys quickly, but Terry intrigued me and kept my interest.

Taking a Gamble in Vegas

Girl meets boy. Girl dates boy. Can girl keep boy? Terry and I continued our long-distance romance, but I felt like I was always so readily available for him whenever he invited me to another city to see him. Everybody likes a challenge, especially a competitive athlete like him. I realized that I needed to be a little less available to keep him on his toes. So that's exactly what I did. I decided that the next time Terry asked me to come to see him, I would tell him no and then surprise him! Sure enough, a few days later, he asked me to come to Vegas and I told him no. After we hung up, I immediately booked a flight, bolted out of the house, and headed to Vegas.

Upon landing at the McCarran Airport, I took a cab directly to the arena where he was wrestling. I arrived there at about seven thirty P.M., and a preliminary match was already under way. His wrestling buddies immediately saw me in the audience and reported back to the Hulkster. I was dressed in a tight dress with long red fingernails and lots of makeup. Let's just say I stood out in a crowd.

To my surprise, Terry didn't seem happy to see me. I began to think I made a terrible mistake and became embarrassed for showing up without calling him first. I felt like I walked in on a party that I wasn't invited to. Then it hit me: *I'm dating Terry exclusively, but maybe he's not dating me exclusively,* I thought. *When I told him I wasn't coming to Vegas, maybe he made plans with another woman.*

Terry and I got along so great that I never stopped to think about the possibility of him being with any other women. I often forgot I was dating a celebrity and about the fact that he probably had girlfriends in other towns. In Terry's defense, we had never spoken about being exclusive. But we had so much fun together and had so much in common, I thought it was just understood. I finally asked Terry if he had other girlfriends. He told me that he didn't and explained that he couldn't get serious with me because he was on the road all the time. I understood.

That night, we went back to Terry's hotel room and made love. Then he fell right to sleep. The following morning when I had to leave to go back to Los Angeles, he didn't even get up to say good-bye. In fact, he never even looked at me. He simply told me that there was a hundred dollars on the table for my airfare back home. *Wow, now I really feel like a call girl,* I thought.

I took a gamble surprising Terry in Vegas and it clearly didn't pay off. Quick tip: Boyfriends don't like girlfriends showing up unexpectedly. When I got back to Los Angeles, I decided I would play a little hard to get with no more surprises. Terry would call the salon and I told the girls to tell him I wasn't there and they didn't know where I was. I became elusive and created some mystery. I really stuck to my guns. And, boy, did it work! Pretty soon he missed having the convenient access to me and all the fun we had together. Terry even asked me to come live with him in Minnesota.

I remembered from working at the nail shop that a lot of the girls complained about getting dumped by their boyfriends soon after they moved in together. Again, it's that old saying, Why buy the cow when you can get the milk for free? In other words, why would the guy ask you to marry him if you're already giving him all that he wants? Moving in with a guy whom you're not married to seems to doom relationships. Well, as far as I was concerned, Terry was going to have to buy the cow. When I told him that I didn't want to move in together, I didn't hear from him for an entire week. *Uh-oh, there goes a perfectly good guy,* I thought. *That's it. We're done.*

A week later, Terry phoned me at the salon and said he needed to talk to me urgently in person. He seemed very serious. He asked me to fly to San Francisco where he was wrestling at the Cow Palace.

I flew up there although I had the feeling that he wanted to break up. I could almost hear him now, "Linda, you're a great girl, but it's not going to work out." *Well, if he's going to dump me,*

I'm going to make it difficult for him, I thought. So I made sure I looked smoking hot, wearing the shortest little leopard-print miniskirt and sexiest heels I owned. Hey, I wasn't going down without a fight!

After the wrestling match, I took a cab with Terry to his hotel room at the Ramada Inn. He seemed nervous in the car and wasn't talking very much. We went to his room, and he asked me to sit on the edge of the bed. He started the conversation by saying, "You'll recall that I mentioned that anybody I was going to marry I had to live with first."

"Yeah," I said, with a nervous gulp.

Terry went on to say that he loved me and that during the past week when he went back home to Florida for a visit, he began thinking about our relationship. He said he also saw his old girlfriend Donna as well as his parents. He explained that he did a lot of soul searching and that he came to a decision. I figured it was at this point that he was building up for the big breakup. He was quiet for a moment, looked me in the eyes, and said, "Linda, I love you. Will you please marry me?" And it was at this point I realized that he was down on bended knee!

"Yes. Yes! I will!" My head was spinning! We hugged and kissed each other. I was so shocked at the turn of events! Here I thought when I was flying up that it would be the last time I saw him. But this was what I'd hoped for and apparently he had too! We didn't want to be apart from each other anymore.

I didn't know what kind of husband Terry would be, but I did know that I had never met anyone who captured and kept my heart as long as he did. I felt like I was constantly learning things with him. I had never been out of the state of California before I met him. Now, I was zipping all over the place! I loved the lifestyle and learning about new people and places with him. I loved his craziness. I loved how we would be rolling down a highway in some random state and out of nowhere he would practice his prematch interview talk that he became famous for. I was amazed by the things Terry would come up with and say on the fly. I loved going to the matches and seeing and hearing the screaming fans. I loved that he was somebody, and I was always proud to be his girl.

Terry also had that southern gentleman quality about him. He was very generous with me and always opened doors. Although we never discussed kids, I knew that I was crazy about him and didn't know exactly what love was. Did I love him? I felt like I did. But what *is* love? You want a finite answer to that, but it never came to me. I just knew that I didn't want to lose Terry. I made my decision that I was willing to go wherever the road took me with him.

After he asked me to marry him, I came home and told my parents. I think they realized that no matter what they said or did, they were not going to force me out of this relationship. They had met Terry on several occasions and also thought he was a southern gentleman and not the persona that he seemed to be in *Rocky III*. My parents trusted my decision. They were excited for me. Terry wanted to ask my parents for their blessing to marry me anyway. He invited them to dinner, and on the way over to the restaurant we stopped by to see my friend Dana, who was also a manicurist, and we changed clothes at her place. We took a shower, and Terry asked me if I could wash his jeans for him. When we came out of the shower and I went to transfer his jeans into the dryer, I found out it was broken! He had to wear wet jeans to the restaurant and was not thrilled about it.

We went to this fabulous English Tudor–style steak restaurant called Bob Burns in Woodland Hills, California. I think my parents knew he was going to ask them. We made small talk and had dinner. Then, Terry said to my father, "I love your daughter and I think she's special. I don't know how I could live without her. I want to marry Linda; do I have your permission?"

My father said, "Yes. I just want you to take care of her. I know you travel on airplanes and I don't want her to get hurt. Please look out for her." I was so surprised to hear how he kind of passed the torch. He was really concerned that Terry would take good care of me. My mother made one point when she said, "Terry, you have to promise to not take our girl away from us. You travel a lot and are from Florida, but she has a big family here and we love her and we don't want her to disappear."

"I promise," Terry responded.

Ring Bells to Wedding Bells

On December 18, 1983, my wedding to Terry was like a scene right out of the circus—the geeks, freaks, midgets, and giants were all in attendance. How could you expect anything less when you're marrying a professional wrestler?

Terry and I created our own guest lists for the wedding and then combined them for one master list that consisted of two hundred people. My list was composed of my big Italian family, wild manicurists, and beach girlfriends. Terry's was a bit different. Although he invited his childhood friends, their spouses, and his family from Florida, he also invited his wrestling family from Minnesota and all points in between. When I looked at the names on Terry's guest list, I immediately knew we were in for one wild wedding reception: Adrian Adonis, Dizzy Hogan, André the Giant, and Bobby "The Brain" Heenan, among others. It was certainly a roundup of colorful characters. Other very important names on Terry's list were wrestling promoter Vince McMahon Jr. and his wife, Linda. Terry had recently signed a contract with Vince, and plans were all set for us to move to New York after the wedding so he could wrestle for the World Wrestling Federation. McMahon seemed to have big plans for expanding the WWF with Terry as the centerpiece. Our marriage marked an important moment for all of us. While Vince had already brought us into his wrestling family, we were now bringing him into ours.

Since Terry spent five years early in his career wrestling professionally in Japan, there were many Japanese guests and dignitaries attending our nuptials. They had an incredible amount of respect for Terry, and he was consistently a big draw over there, mainly because of his flowing blond hair and size. They worshipped Hulk Hogan just like he was a sumo wrestler. Before we got married, Terry flew me to Japan. The first day there, I wore my hair in two pigtails, and a lot of photographs were taken of me like that. After we got married, I saw a lot of cartoon drawings of Terry and me in Japanese magazines. They always depicted me with those blond pigtails. I guess my two pigtails, orange lips, and orange nails were my thing.

With all of Terry's time spent in Japan, it certainly made sense that Terry would invite his Japanese friends and wrestling colleagues to California for the ceremony. Now, we all know that the Japanese love cameras, right? Well, the Japanese at our wedding were no exception. A Japanese film crew of eight showed up ready to film all of the action from start to finish. Hulk Hogan was a big star in Japan, and their big star was getting married. That added up to major news for them! The legendary Japanese wrestling champion, Antonio Inoki, attended our wedding and, along with Terry, gave me a special gift before the ceremony. They each handed me a velvet gift box, and inside each one was a beautiful and breathtaking strand of real pearls. I wore both strands on the big day and felt just like Jackie O.

The necklaces matched my beautiful wedding dress, which had pearls all over it. The dress also had long lace sleeves and a veil that flowed behind me, almost twenty feet long. I wore cute white ankle strap shoes and tucked into my bra was a blue hankie, which was my grandmother's and intended to bring me good luck. Last, I wore a sexy garter with a little touch of red and green on it to celebrate the Christmas holiday season.

My mom fixed my hair with my sister, aunts, and grand-mother looking on. Once I was ready, we all hopped in the limo together to go to the church, which was a beautiful cathedral. From the pipe organ to the hand-carved crucifixes to the large stained-glass windows, I was certain it would be a marriage made in heaven. The church was built in the 1800s in the heart of Hollywood, California. Yep, another Hollywood marriage. So I guess I *am* a Hollywood wife.

Terry and I said our vows, and I believed that doing so in the eyes of God would somehow help him live up to them. I truly believed Terry when he accepted the vows read by the priest and said, "I do." He placed a beautiful three-carat pear-shaped dia-mond on my left hand, and I placed a beautiful gold nugget–style ring with three diamonds on his. The three diamonds signified *Rocky III*. After all, that's where I first saw him.

Terry and I kissed, then happily walked the great length of the church to the crush of people outside who tossed rice at us. Wrestlers have big hands, so when seven-foot-four André the Giant tosses rice at you, it's like a snowstorm! We got in the back of the limo, dusted ourselves off, and immediately popped a bottle of champagne, which awaited us on ice. We toasted the start of our brand-new life together as husband and wife. To the world we were now Mr. and Mrs. Hulk Hogan. To our families, we were Mr. and Mrs. Terry Bollea. To us, soul mates.

It was like a fairy tale come true.

Terry and I were whisked off in the stretch limo to our wedding party, which was at the Westwood Marquis (now the W Hotel) in Westwood, California. We had an absolute blast! Hulk, André, and the other wrestlers held the bar up all night long. I remember the band played "New York, New York," which was soon to be our new home. Terry and I took the dance floor alone as everyone looked on with glee in their eyes. Then I tossed the bouquet, which my friend Dana caught. Terry also had to remove my garter in front of the crowd. The sexy stripper music kicked in, and to everyone's surprise Terry got down on one knee and pulled it off . . . with his teeth! The guests screamed, laughed, and applauded just as though he was in the wrestling ring. A true performer.

At the end of the night when Terry carried me over the threshold of our hotel suite, I felt like the luckiest girl in the world. I had ordered some room service and was getting out of my wedding dress when there was a knock at the door. *Room service is here already?* I thought. I opened the door and to my complete surprise, it was my mom. "Is everything okay?" I asked, surprised.

"The wrestlers have been down there drinking all night, and they want me to pay the bar tab, which is twelve thousand dollars," she said. "I don't have the cash or a credit card to cover that."

I felt for my mom, and she had no choice but to ask Terry for the money. That really upset him. He was going to take care of me from the wedding night on, but he felt that the party was a send-off and the bride's parents should cover it. I understood that. My mother understood that. And my family understood that. However, it was a bad situation, and I know my mom felt sorry for asking, but she had no other choice. Terry tossed his wallet to me and generously came to the rescue. I felt bad for him, but my mother did plan and pay for the entire wedding despite the fact that her house had burned down just two months before. My mother apologized profusely and kissed me good-bye.

After my mother left, I went into the bathroom and changed into a sexy negligee. When I came out Terry had fallen asleep, so drunk and tired that he still had steak in his mouth. Not exactly what wedding night dreams are made of.

Chapter Four

COAST TO COAST

FEW MONTHS BEFORE TERRY AND I GOT MARRIED, Vince McMahon Jr. and Terry reunited by phone again. Vince Jr. called with an offer we couldn't refuse. He flew out to our condo in Minnesota to talk about a new business opportunity with his company the World Wrestling Federation (WWF).

Terry was really putting his name on the map in Minnesota as a wrestler to be reckoned with. Then, with the further exposure from appearing in the *Rocky III* movie, Terry's star was definitely on the rise. There was no doubt that Vince had a keen sense of business and noticed the attention on the Hulk. He was always ten steps ahead of the other promoters and a genius when it came to marketing and television. Vince and his wife, Linda, would eventually take this business from small, dingy, dimly lit no-name arenas with fifty to one hundred people in the audience to a billion-dollar, multimedia, worldwide company.

Vince knew that Terry was his golden boy, and Terry soon became his golden goose by becoming the front man for the WWF.

When Vince first came to Minnesota to meet with Terry, Terry asked me to pick Vince up at the airport while he showered after a wrestling match. Vince was tall with a commanding presence, just like his wrestlers. He was also charismatic, with a great announcer's voice. Vince recognized me instantly. He introduced himself and gave me a big hug. On the way back to the condo, we made conversation, which mainly consisted of talking about the old days working with Terry. When we got to our place, Vince and Terry got along great. They sat in the living room together for hours, hard at work mapping out a plan. From the laughs coming out of the living room while I worked in the kitchen, it was clear that they acted like no time had passed and they definitely seemed excited by the new plans.

They eventually invited me into the living room to speak with me about their business ideas. They also wanted to see if I was up for us doing what Vince needed us to do. It was clear that there was not only going to be a lot of traveling to matches in different cities, but there were going to be many photo shoots, interviews, live television, and marketing meetings in order to put wrestling on the map. It seemed like it was going to be a constant flow of work with no time off.

I thought it was very impressive that Terry considered my opinion on such an important decision, even though we were not married quite yet. I have always had an adventurous streak in me, and it surely sounded like an adventure to work with Vince and the WWF. After Terry drove Vince back to the airport and came home, he looked me in the eye and said, "Linda, do you realize how big this is going to be? Are you ready to make a run through New York?"

I had been with Terry in and out of different wrestling events for the whole year before we got married, so I was very familiar with wrestling and the business. I didn't feel strange or like a stranger to it. I was actually excited about going to New York, because I had heard all about it but had never been there. For me, to think that I would be living near New York City was like a crazy dream. I wasn't lonely moving to New York City, because I had lived alone in my own apartment for quite some time and was used to it. It wasn't scary saying good-bye to my family, either, because Terry and I had traveled all the time. We were always back and forth. The weird part for me was not having to get up every morning to go to a job. From the time I was fifteen years old, I had always worked. It was strange being taken care of and just hanging out. But I knew Terry wanted to build a life with me, and I only wanted to keep him in his business as he was now the sole breadwinner.

At that point, when we were presented with the opportunity to leave Minnesota, I knew how smart Terry was and how he was a figurehead in his field. He earned the most money out of all the wrestlers, and when he said we would make one more run through New York, I knew it would probably be more of the same, just more intense! So the idea of long hours and hard work didn't even ruffle me. I was in!

Now that we were going to be married, we felt that if this was an opportunity to make more money and a better life for ourselves, then we should do it! I could also see inside of Terry that he really wanted to make a go of this. He just wasn't sure if I was ready for what was to come. But I'm pretty tough and can see myself through just about any situation that's put in front of me. I was clearly a good support mechanism for Terry, and I really looked forward to all of the new stuff we were going to experience together in New York.

"Let's do it! Let's go for it!" I responded.

"Well, it's going to be a lot of work."

I never imagined just how much work actually lay ahead.

Soon after our wedding, we moved as a new husband and wife to Stamford, Connecticut, which was (and still is) the headquarters of Vince's business organization, now the WWE.

When we arrived, we first stayed with our good friends Peggy and David Schultz. David aka "Dr. D" was a wrestler who previously worked in Tennessee. While Terry was busy taking meetings and doing photo shoots at the WWF studios in Stamford, I busied myself with a local real estate agent looking for a new apartment. It was a bit difficult to find something. Everything on the East Coast was so old, crowded, or in the middle of nowhere. In the meantime, Terry and I also stayed at a Howard Johnson's Motor Lodge on the side of the highway in Stamford for six weeks until we moved in. Terry had been close friends since childhood with Brutus "The Barber" Beefcake. So he brought him into the WWF as well. Brutus ended up coming to Connecticut and staying with us in our hotel room. Two's company and three's a crowd, so I made sure "The Barber" got cut out of our room pretty quickly. I wasn't trying to come between them, but in such close quarters I needed my privacy with my husband.

I had to put up with a lot—the laundry, suitcases, bills, traveling, not really having my own life or friends. But it was okay. I liked being on the road and hanging with other gals who were sort of in the same position. It was a time of change and growth—everyone in the biz understood that and we were all trying to make it work! At the time, it was just our lifestyle and I accepted it. Sure, his wrestling buddies were always around, but I liked a little privacy for Terry and me every once in a while. I enjoyed being a support mechanism for him. We were building his career together on the road. It wasn't what a wrestling wife was supposed to do; it was what I wanted to do. I just liked being his lady.

Terry got a rare few days off, and we eventually found a place we could call home together. It was a three-story town house at 101 Seaside Avenue in Stamford. It was brand-new, but the other houses and the street were old and looked like something out of *All in the Family*. Along with the cold winter weather, it was a very different lifestyle from what I was used to in Los Angeles, that's for sure. When we moved into the new town house in Connecticut, I fixed it up cute and wanted to make a nice home life for us. I did it inexpensively and chose to hunt at antique shops for most of the furniture. I even made my own curtains with iron-on tape as I can't sew a stitch! I enjoyed fixing up the house and finding new stuff in a strange town. I tried to host nice parties and was always Miss Congeniality to Terry's wrestling buddies who would come to town and usually stay with us instead of in some crappy hotel.

For the most part, I loved fulfilling my role as wife to Hulk Hogan, and when we lived in Connecticut, I would happily cook for the guys and make any visitors we had welcome. Of course there were some minor bumps along the way as I settled into newlywed life. The following story tells about one such bump.

It was really hard to find good food on the road, so when the wrestlers came back home they appreciated a fresh, healthy meal. Remember, these guys have to keep a lot of weight on—lots of protein foods to build muscle, like chicken and steak, fresh vegetables, and salad. Linda McMahon had told me about a great seafood restaurant in Greenwich, so I drove there and picked up some fresh, raw shrimp. The guy who worked there packed them in ice for me and put them in the back of my car. I went shopping, forgot about the shrimp, and by the time I got home the ice had melted. I didn't know you needed to keep shrimp super iced down or it could go bad, so I cooked all of the shrimp along with some New York steaks. Terry and Brutus ate the hell out of it! They literally were licking their fingers it was so good. That night, they had to wrestle each other somewhere up near Boston, which was driving distance from where we lived. By the time they drove to the arena and hit the dressing room, they had started showing symptoms of food poisoning. That night Terry and Brutus were locked up in the ring, worried about shitting themselves in front of thousands of fans. This was an elimination match—literally.

● ● ●

WE WERE ONE OF THE FEW WRESTLING COUPLES WHO ACTUALLY lived in Connecticut near the office. Terry's position within the WWF was demanding. Vince would have him constantly doing television interviews and photo shoots in between his matches, so living close made sense. In the wrestling business you never sold your home and moved to the new territory. That would kind of make you look desperate and show the promoter that he didn't have to work as hard to make you happy to keep you there. You live there! But with a contract in place, we felt like we could settle in Connecticut and really give it a go with the WWF.

Vince was planning a big match for January 23, 1984, between Hulk Hogan and the Iron Sheik for the Heavyweight Championship belt at Madison Square Garden in New York City. We all know *now* how the wrestling business operates, but back then it was extremely covert. I didn't know what was going to happen that night, and it was never explained to me.

There was incredible hype leading up to the match. Terry was on a whirlwind publicity tour weeks in advance. Vince and his wife, Linda, were very thankful that Terry and I put ourselves on the line and didn't take a honeymoon after our wedding. We got right down to work without missing a beat. And when I say "we didn't miss a beat," I mean it. Terry was completely dedicated and totally focused, and I stayed by his side. We traveled so much together that I didn't care that we missed having a honeymoon. We worked out, drove, ate, and spent every night together in hotels. It was our way of life and we did it together. The only thing different was that I never climbed into the ring!

That night, Mrs. McMahon let me sit in the owner's box with her and not with the rest of the fans like I usually did. It was clearly a big step up.

When Hulk beat the Iron Sheik, history was made. The crowd cheered for fifteen minutes straight. Terry had a lot of devoted fans and believers. I will never forget that night. I was very proud of him.

Back then, Terry and I were very much a couple. We were lovers and best friends. We had a great relationship and rarely fought. He was always excited to see me sitting out in the audience watching him do his thing. As he got more famous, I was still sitting on the sidelines watching it all and rooting him on. And we continued to do everything together. Terry and I shared it all and did a lot of laughing in the old days, living life together one day at a time.

Wrestling Wives

We've all heard of football wives, baseball wives, and basketball wives. However, there was a new breed of sports wives on the rise in the mid-1980s—"wrestling wives."

Wrestling wives are the emotional support mechanism for the wrestlers. Not to mention, we are sexy and fun! The wrestlers' demanding schedule of training and travel was just as grueling as their matches. Most wives didn't travel because a lot of them had families at home.

I was one of the only wives who actually traveled from city to city. Some of the wives would show up in various cities, if the match was near their hometown or took place on a weekend. But I spent days on the road with Terry, driving thousands of miles in a rental car or flying coach class to each city until we had a day off. Then we would go home to Connecticut for two or three days. It was laundry, gym, tan, grocery store, bills, and sleep. Most of the time that we were on the road, we would get to a city and go to the gym and then the arena. At six P.M. I would say "good luck" as he went into the locker room (a place I *rarely* went) with the guys. Sweaty guys taping their wrists, fingers, knees, and elbows. I had no idea what they were doing, but tensions ran high in the locker room as they prepared for the big fight.

I would sit backstage, usually on a forklift or out in the bleachers, as the crowd began to enter the building. Over the years, I'd made friends with building managers and referees, but I really didn't have anyone to talk to. However, there were always other girls who would show up. They were one-night stands that the wrestlers called "Ring Rats." They were obsessive fans who dreamed of being with one of the wrestlers. I never wanted to be thought of in that way and tried to keep to myself.

Of course, I didn't have to travel with Terry, but I wanted to; and he needed the help and support. I tried my best to hang with him on the road. Remember, this was in the early stages of wrestling, and it was growing at an alarming rate! During the meet and greets with the fans, I would be in the background laying out more pictures to be autographed, helping to organize lines for the kids, or just speaking to them and their parents while they waited in long lines to get a few seconds with their heroes. I also made sure Terry had all the right clothes for the events he needed to attend. If he had a meeting immediately following a match, I made sure I brought an outfit for him to wear. It took both of us working as a team to succeed on the road.

I always enjoyed traveling to the Philadelphia Spectrum because I got an opportunity to see one of my favorite promoters,

Arnold Skaaland, and his lovely wife, Betty. She was a classy New York Italian woman in her fifties with a golden tan and platinum blond hair pulled straight back into a bun. I remember thinking I finally found someone to talk to. Greg "The Hammer" Valentine's first wife would hang, too. They were nice companions to talk to while the wrestling matches were going on. It was great because I was on the road alone with Terry so much of the time.

I connected with many of the wrestlers' wives on a personal level because we were all in the same boat, although I was the only wife who went to every city. However, it was clear that I wasn't the wife of just *any* wrestler. I was the wife of the reigning heavyweight champion of the world. I realized that along with that came a responsibility, and I always stood by my man. I didn't want to be a quitter. After all, he couldn't quit. Besides, what would I do? Sit home and wait? Work at the mall? School wasn't my thing. I really loved being with him, and he needed my support and companionship.

Throughout the years, especially early on, I tried to assist Terry creatively with establishing his image. When I had first moved from California to Minnesota, I remember one night I was cutting up a T-shirt in the kitchen. It was a shocking pink men's extra-large tee—totally loud, yet totally cool. I folded the shirt as if it were a paper doll and I cut into it leaving a ribbed, shredded sort of see-through look. It immediately caught Terry's eye. "Hold on a minute," he said. "What are you doing to that shirt? Let me try it on."

"You want to try it on? Okay," I responded, handing it over.

Terry put on the T-shirt and even though it fit him extremely snug, he loved what it did for his body. He could see his biceps, abs, and lats through the shredded cotton. The shreds made him look like the Incredible Hulk busting out of his clothes. Terry stood in front of the mirror admiring himself. "I like it!" he exclaimed.

This was the start of Terry shredding the back of his red-and-yellow Hulkamania T-shirts. For five years straight, I can't even tell you how many T-shirts I cut up and shredded for him. Thank God the shirts were eventually mass-produced! Terry's style of wearing a bandanna has some interesting origins as well. When we were in California together riding Harleys, his long blond hair was always blowing in his face. My father took off his bandanna and tied it on Terry's head. Terry instantly dug the look; it was a sort of easy rider/bad boy vibe that definitely worked for him. After that, one of Terry's trademarks was wearing a bandanna; and whenever he tore it off in the ring, the crowd went crazy!

Terry was no suit-and-tie guy. When we attended meetings, Terry would wow the executives with his wrestler sense of style. And I was with him at every meeting. Terry usually wore cowboy boots, a pair of boot-cut tight jeans, a big western belt buckle, and a tight-ass T-shirt showing off his big, tan, lotioned-down arms. He needed to retain a gimmick, so to speak, and wearing a suit and tie like the rest of the business executives wasn't the way to go. Terry was a superstar, so it didn't matter if he wore his pajamas when he met executives from toy or video companies. However, even though Terry dressed down in jeans and casual attire, I had to dress on the same level as the rest of the other businesspeople. For instance, I would wear a St. John knit top and slacks, along with a beautiful coat and purse. I needed to look the part of a successful businesswoman. I feel that if people see the wife of a celebrity behind the scenes and she's put together, they know what the star is really all about. He was Hulk Hogan the wrestler, but Terry was also a brilliant businessman who was making the big bucks, and many individuals wanted to rub up against him.

AFTER TERRY WON THE TITLE, THE NEXT REALLY BIG EVENT SCHEDuled was *Wrestlemania I* for March 31, 1985, at Madison Square Garden. Sure the wrestlers had muscle, but Vince's marketing muscle was the driving force in preparing for this enormous event. He was turning his cigar-box wrestling into family entertainment.

The wrestling wives needed to step up their game for the event as well. After all, this was the Academy Awards of wrestling—the very best matches, the biggest crowd, and worldwide media attention. It was my idea for the wrestling wives to wear black gowns with long gloves and treat this like a red carpet event. TV cameras, celebrities, limos—the truth was that Terry was really a television star!

I'd like to think I had a lot to do with changing the image of how people perceived wrestling and the wrestlers outside of the ring. When people saw Terry and me walk out onto a red carpet dressed in classy black-tie fashion, I think fans looked at him a bit differently. Sometimes fans even asked me for my autograph. *Who am I?* I thought. *I'm just Hulk's wife.* I didn't realize how big of a star Terry was becoming.

•   ·   •

THINGS BECAME SIGNIFICANTLY DIFFERENT IN TERRY'S LIFE. HE got so popular, so famous, so fast—and I watched his fame grow every day. We tried to keep our private life private. However, it was starting to get almost impossible to do the simple things that we normally did, like going to the gym, grocery store, and tanning salon. We couldn't even go out of the house without people noticing him from the car window at a traffic light and going nuts. Fans began to bang on our front door, fan mail poured in, and people would follow us at the mall.

The fame that came with being married to Terry wasn't something I was prepared for at the beginning. I'm very happy that it happened, and I'm proud of him for working so hard to make it happen, but it was constant work even when he wasn't on the job. If we were walking through an airport, sometimes tired from a long flight, people would often follow us. And they didn't just recognize Terry and then whisper to their friends, "Hey, it's Hulk Hogan." No, they had to come up to him, meet him, and touch him. It was as if they had to touch this larger-than-life character to believe they actually just met him.

I had to develop a thick skin very quickly as a wrestling wife because it wasn't just the kids and their parents who approached him. No, it was women, too. Whether they were hotel clerks, flight attendants, or bank tellers, I had to deal with women chasing after him all the time. You couldn't rent a car without all of the girls who worked there coming out from behind the counter to meet him. I kind of got used to it though and realized it was just another part of the business. Show business! Looking back, the women's attention made all the sense in the world. Terry was tall, handsome, and muscular. Not to mention superfamous and now super-rich.

I remember trying to pay some of our bills on an airplane and realized I had missed our rent payment the past three months in a row. I desperately needed help organizing our expenses. Somebody from the WWF hooked me up with a real estate broker. She said she knew the principal of a local school who could help us with our bills and accounting. When I met him, I literally handed him a paper grocery bag filled with all of our bills. I told him to call me and let me know what was happening. With his help, Terry and I finally got things in order. We had so many checks coming in so fast that I couldn't count them all. I would just hand them over to our new bookkeeper, and he would deposit them into our account. After a couple of months working with him, he called me and said, "I hope you're having a nice day because I have some good news for you."

"What's going on?" I asked.

"You have a million dollars in your bank account."

Terry had only been with the WWF for a little over a year. It was hard to register that this was real. I was happy that we made it, but I also realized how much work it took to get us there. Quite honestly, Terry and I didn't even have time to spend it. We didn't live much differently than before. We still drove the same beat-up car and stayed in crappy hotels. Even though Terry was the face of the WWF, we chose to stay at the same hotel as the other wrestlers. As far as we were concerned, you stayed where they stayed, you ate where they ate, and you traveled the way they traveled. This created a good camaraderie between all of us. We were all in this together and treated it that way.

Tan, Ready, and Rested

Wrestlemania III on March 29, 1987, was another star-studded spectacle. Even though I was from California, I'd never met big celebrities in person besides Farrah Fawcett. Vince would have celebrities attend every Wrestlemania. I was backstage with all of these stars, such as Alice Cooper and Aretha Franklin. My husband was now a star himself! For the main event, Hulk Hogan put his World Championship belt on the line against André the Giant. Hulk ended up slamming the giant. The crowd roared like I'd never heard before. I was so proud of my husband I cried! We celebrated. It was such a special feeling when Terry and I hugged after the match. We had come so far. He was the nation's hero, and he was my hero.

But all that time traveling on the road with Terry, I finally felt like *I* had been body slammed. During one year we spent 324 days on the road! For the longest time, Terry and I never spent a holiday at home. Every Christmas, Thanksgiving, and Easter we were at a different wrestling event. I had flown to so many cities, sat in so many arenas, washed so many yellow tights and boots, eaten in so many fast-food places, stayed in so many motels, and partied so many late nights that I was done. And I looked it. I had major breakouts on my face from lack of sleep and stress. I missed my period for eight solid months while I was still taking the pill. My hair was dry and brittle even though I didn't even color it then. I was sleep deprived and more tired than I had ever been before in my life. I experienced the kind of total exhaustion that would cause most people to rethink their lives. I was going to self-destruct. I needed to find Linda again.

Meanwhile, the wrestling business grew at a staggering pace, and we realized Terry couldn't take a break, even if he wanted to. I, on the other hand, needed to take one for the both of us. Sure, being on the road was an essential part of being married to a wrestler. Just as it was for people on circus, carnival, and rock-and-roll concert tours, the road was our home. However, it was time to establish a *real* home base.

One of the things we did do with our money was buy a three-bedroom town house in Redington Beach, Florida. We could easily fly from Connecticut in under three hours and be guaranteed warm sunny weather. We had spent so many days out of every year in gloomy cold cities during the winter. I needed to be in the sunshine once again. And when Terry would get a few days off and he'd come to Florida, it was like we were newlyweds all over again. I made sure I was tan, ready, and rested when he showed up.

With Terry on the road and me at home it put a different spin on our relationship. Now I had to get used to being alone a lot of the time. I would watch him on TV. He would call me every night. He would call me every morning. But it wasn't the same thing as being with him. Sure, I missed him. However, I knew I needed a change. I also knew how hard Terry worked, so when he came home, whatever he wanted to do was fine with me.

When Terry was home, a lot of his wrestling buddies came down to Florida to hang out as well. Because he was the leader of the wrestlers, the party was always at our house. I'd throw barbecues together at the last minute. That's when I invented the "Company Cupboard." I took one big shelf out of my pantry and piled it with the typical party food. Peanuts, chips, sodas, beer—you name it, they ate it. I was always stocked up. Some of my favorite recipes were invented in those days. Here are a couple of my standards.

CITY CHICKEN

There is no chicken in this recipe, but the skewers will look like drumsticks when they're finished.

2 cups seasoned bread crumbs
½ cup parmesan cheese
¼ cup chopped parsley
2 to 3 eggs, beaten
2 pounds veal, cubed
2 pounds pork, cubed
garlic salt and pepper (to taste)
olive oil for frying

Preheat oven to 350 degrees. In one bowl, mix together the bread crumbs, parmesan cheese, and parsley. In a separate bowl beat the eggs. Dip the meat pieces into the egg batter, soaking the meat on all sides; then roll each piece in the bread crumb mixture. Stick the pieces of cubed meat onto skewers, alternating veal and pork. Sprinkle with garlic salt and pepper.

In a large pan, fry the skewers in olive oil on all sides until the meat is golden brown. Then drain each skewer on paper towel. Place the skewers in a roasting pan and bake in the oven for 1 hour.

CROCK POT HAM

1 8-pound ham with bone (pre-cooked)
2 8-ounce cans apple pie filling
1 cup honey
1 cup cinnamon sugar

Put the ham in the slow cooker. Pour the apple pie filling, honey, and cinnamon sugar all over the ham. Cook on high for 4 to 5 hours.

The ham will fall off the bone, and the gravy is amazing!

I think being the wind beneath Terry's wings was my forte, my calling. Terry was the wrestler . . . the showman. You stick a camera in his face and he can talk at the drop of a hat. Me, not so much. I was content with being behind the scenes. Sure, I was a celebrity in my own right just being married to Hulk Hogan. But Terry was the star, and I was fine with that. I was always very proud of him and thrilled to be his wife.

As far as the World Wrestling Federation was concerned, we were one big family. However, when I turned twenty-seven years old, I felt Terry and I should begin building our own little federation at home.

It was time to start a family.

Chapter Five

OH BABY!

ULK HOGAN WAS A HERO TO SO MANY KIDS. The WWF always collaborated with different charitable organizations benefiting children, specifically the Make-A-Wish Foundation and the Starlight Children's Foundation. These groups work with terminally ill children and grant them their dying wishes. And it was amazing to me how many kids shared the same wish—to meet Hulk Hogan in person. So many kids with such little time left looked up from their wheelchairs, hospital beds, and parents' arms at Hulk, who brought a little magic into their lives.

Terry was so powerful, yet gentle around those little angels. And he always had a kind word for their parents, who were saints. I always stood by his side hugging the kids and giving them T-shirts and bandannas, gifts from the Hulkster.

From watching Terry deal as warmly as he did with these ill children, I knew he'd be a great dad. I was more than ready to be a parent, and I think he was ready, too. Now that Terry had become so successful, and I knew he was on his way, I felt it was time for us to take a moment and put down some real family roots.

It took a little while, but about six months into trying to conceive, I got pregnant. I remember Terry looking at the positive pregnancy test in the kitchen. His eyes lit up. He couldn't believe it. Yep, I was pregnant! We went to the doctor, and the pregnancy was taking off and doing well. We were on our way to becoming parents!

About four months along, Terry and I went to a wrestling match he had on his schedule in Rhode Island. We drove from Connecticut to Rhode Island in the dead of winter. It was so cold that despite the car heater being on, the frigid air still managed to seep in.

Terry was in the dressing room getting ready to go out and wrestle when I suddenly got cramps, bad ones. I didn't know why. I thought maybe it was growing pains from the baby because I was almost midway through my pregnancy. I rushed to the ladies' room, sat down on the toilet, and blood gushed from my body. I realized I was having a miscarriage. I was devastated. Terry must have sensed something was wrong because he came into the public restroom to check on me. He was so tall that he looked over the stall and saw me sitting on the toilet crying.

An ambulance was called and I was taken to a local hospital where they announced that there was no baby. It was an ectopic pregnancy, which means the pregnancy occurred outside the uterus.

"I thought I was four and a half months' pregnant," I said to the nurse.

"No, I'm sorry," she responded. "But you can try again."

It took so long to get pregnant the first time that maybe I can't have a baby, I thought. *Maybe I'm not meant to have a child.* After a few months, Terry and I started again. Six months later, and voilà! Preggers! This time it took and I was ecstatic. I began seeing Dr. Lewis at the All Women's Center in Tampa, Florida, where we monitored the pregnancy closely.

The second time around I told no one I was pregnant except Terry. I didn't want to jinx it. I stayed home, didn't work out, and ate and ate and ate. I didn't care about anything except the baby. During this time, I lived at our home in Florida so I wouldn't catch a cold up north. I was tan, healthy, and very pregnant. I was having the Hulkster's baby and it showed. I was huge! I thought for certain it was a boy. In fact, I prepared the nursery for a boy. I was so big that I looked like I was smuggling watermelons. The normal thing that happens during pregnancy is that the baby drops. Mine kept growing straight out in front of me.

I wrote an entry in my journal on March 4, 1988, which is exactly two months and one day before I delivered Brooke. I clearly had the baby blues:

> *Well I'm having a bad day. I just keep crying because I'm so depressed. Terry won't be home for five more days. He doesn't like making love to me anymore because I'm so fat and pregnant. I have no more self-esteem left. I hate look-ing at myself in the mirror. Today I weigh 183 pounds!*

The veins in the back of my knees are having blow-outs. My feet are totally swollen. I can't wear high heels anymore. Maybe Terry can loan me his wrestling boots! I can't exercise now. I'm not tan. I'm sick of staying home. I wish I could go away with Terry just for a couple of days and go out at night. I still have two more months of being pregnant left and it feels more like two years!

It wasn't easy being alone in Florida during my pregnancy with Brooke. Terry's parents were older and traveling was difficult for them, so we didn't see them that much. My family was three thousand miles away in California. This was the first grandchild in my family in many years and it was a special time that I wished they were experiencing with me.

Terry wrestled often during that course of time and watched my baby bump grow. When the baby started kicking, he liked to feel my tummy. We would also read baby books together. He was very excited about becoming a dad for the first time. Terry really loved me, and the child growing inside of me was an extension of our love.

As my due date approached, I got into mommy mode. I fixed up the nursery, washed the quilt, bought stuffed animals, packed the diaper bag, got the changing table ready, and put the car seat in the Suburban. Now, we just needed the kid!

My mom and sister flew from California to Florida for my due date of April 28, 1988, but there was no birth. No labor pains. No dropping. No signs. There was just a lot of kicking and moving. I started to think that if they didn't get this kid out of me soon, I was going to burst! I was pretty uncomfortable, with my measurements topping out at bust 42½, waist 43½, and hips 42½. Pretty soon King Kong Bundy was going to look like a runway model next to me.

Ten more days went by, and finally my mom got worried and called Dr. Lewis.

He told us to come in to see him, but not to worry because a lot of first babies are born late. We gathered our purses and headed to the doctor's office right away. Terry went out on his boat, and my sister stayed behind.

When we got to Dr. Lewis's office, he told me that the baby was in fetal distress. He immediately broke my water and called the hospital, telling them to get ready for me because the baby was coming right then! I was nervous to push this enormous baby out from inside of me. Wouldn't you be?

Terry raced to the hospital. I was going to give birth via C-section. I had to get an epidural. It was a big needle and I was very nervous. Terry showed up right before my epidural. I felt so much better when he got there. I remember his large tan hands tenderly holding mine. It made all the difference in the world to me.

On May 5, 1988, I gave birth to a ten-pound, eight-ounce beautiful and healthy baby girl. What? A girl? I was sure it was going to be a boy. She seemed as big as a two-year-old. Our daughter was adorable with the biggest and brightest eyes, a cute nose like a Smurf, and lungs like . . . well, a singer.

The next challenge was for Terry and me to come up with a name for this angel. With our last name being Bollea, I wanted something simple. It was springtime and she was such a breath of fresh air that I called her Brooke. Her dad nicknamed her Brookeitini. I nicknamed her Brooklyn from when we lived in Connecticut so close to New York. The name fit her perfectly.

Brooke was the most celebrated baby. I had so many flowers in the room from friends and fans who knew that Hulk Hogan was a new dad. It was clear that she was a daddy's girl.

Whatever has transpired in Terry's life—divorce, injuries, whatever—I can bank on the fact that the best thing he ever did was have children. He loves his kids to death, and they have always been the apples of his eye. When Brooke was born, I think that having a daughter got Terry more in touch with the softer side of himself. One time when Brooke started to cry, nothing I could do would stop it, but as soon as Terry picked her up she immediately calmed down. He was gently patting her back when suddenly a man-sized belch came out of our baby girl. I had forgotten to burp her! He loved being a dad.

Innocent Until Proven Guilty

After Brooke's arrival into the world, things seemed perfect between Terry and me. Even though he was traveling for work and couldn't be involved with the family as much as I would've liked him to be, he was a great dad. I missed Terry, but I also understood Hulkamania was still hitting the world like a tidal wave, and our plan was to ride that wave.

Terry had branched out into acting in movies, TV shows, and commercials. He often had to go on location for a lengthy time. On one particular job, he had been gone for almost a month, and I couldn't wait to fly there and visit him. However, I was grounded in Florida until Brooke was old enough to fly.

When Brooke turned four months old, we headed for the set. A car picked us up at the airport and took us to the location where Terry greeted us with a big hug. He took us on a tour of the set and introduced us to all of the people working alongside him.

I really didn't know much about the project Terry was working on or who his costars were. When he introduced me to one of the women on the set, I felt a strange vibe. I can't explain it, but my husband was much more comfortable around everyone else on the film set except her. When we were in her presence, there was definitely a different energy.

She was a tall, young, thin woman with black hair and fair skin—you know, one of those actresses who never went in the sun. When I met her, she was dressed in tight jeans and a white tank top with her nipples protruding evenly and upwardly. (I was nursing and mine were protruding unevenly and downwardly!) I had no reason to mistrust Terry, but I had that intuition and I can't explain it. Think about it—a bunch of people on a set, stuck in a random city in a random hotel, bored and lonely. All of these people are away from their significant others—husbands or wives—on location for months at a time.

As the stay-at-home spouse, you can't escape the thought of it because you read something about men on the set being unfaithful in almost every tabloid. They say while the cat's away the mice will play. Unless you have a devotion to honor the commitment that you made with your spouse, which I did. But I had my doubts about Terry. Maybe it was me being paranoid. Maybe it was my woman's intuition, but I couldn't help how I felt.

I can't say anything happened because I had no proof of my suspicions. In fact, after I arrived home in Florida, I talked myself out of feeling the way I did. *It's the baby blues*, I thought.

I'm overweight, insecure, and my hormones are out of whack. Terry and I are different. He would never do something like that to me.

As the wife of a wrestler I had to get used to some things. And as Terry's career grew, and he became a worldwide celebrity and a household name, it became more difficult. It was constant work and travel. With national celebrity, there was a whole new level of learning, trust, and understanding that I had to have for my husband.

I decided to let the whole negative thing go and be positive.

I LOVED BEING WITH OUR BEAUTIFUL BABY IN OUR NEW HOME IN Clearwater, Florida. During this time, Terry and I spoke about having a second child. He explained that he wanted to wait. I was enjoying and getting used to my new role of mommy, so I was in no rush either.

We all know what they say about the best-laid plans. I ended up forgetting to take my birth control pill on time. At first, I didn't think that missing my pill would be a problem. It took so long to get pregnant with Brooke that I thought we were sure to wrestle a bit with conceiving Hogan baby number two. Plus, Terry was rarely home! Well, I thought wrong. When my period didn't come for two months straight, I decided it was time to take a pregnancy test.

My mom's mom, Grandma Nini (as I liked to call her), had come to visit Brooke and me in Florida. It was great to have my grandmother around for some extra support and help. I told her that I might be pregnant again, but we needed proof. I took a pregnancy test. After we both watched it turn pink, Nini watched me turn white. I was pregnant and afraid to tell Terry. Sure, we had spoken about waiting to have another child, but now that I was pregnant, what was I going to do? I knew Terry was on his way home and would arrive the next day, so I waited to tell him in person. In the meantime, I asked my grandma to keep it a secret.

The next day Terry didn't even make it all the way through the front door before Nini blurted out, "Don't you have something you want to tell him?" (Quick tip: Loud Italian grandmothers can't keep secrets.) I then told Terry that I was pregnant again.

"Why did you tell Nini before you told me?" he asked.

"Why does that matter?" I responded.

"How far along are you?"

"I'm not sure."

Terry was angry, and he took me upstairs for a private chat. He explained that he thought that we were in agreement about waiting to have another child. He felt that this wasn't the right time for him to be a father again, that he didn't even know if he wanted another kid. I really didn't understand his anger about this, since he loved Brooke so much. He punished me by giving me the silent treatment the rest of that night. I got upset and began to cry.

The next morning, Terry seemed like he had a change of heart, but that would soon fade. He kept repeating that he thought we were going to wait. At that point, what did it matter? We had a baby growing inside of me and we loved having a family. This was God's way.

Although my pregnancy with Nick came as a surprise to

Terry, at some point he needed to get over it. Brooke was so beautiful, and I knew that having a second child was going to be just as awesome. But Terry seemed afraid. I guess it was going to be harder for him to come and go as he pleased, and he would have more responsibility on his shoulders. At that time, he was probably going to have to curtail some of the shit he was doing that I didn't know about.

As months went by, surprisingly he never really warmed up to the idea of having another child. I think Terry thought I planned the pregnancy, but I didn't. With the chaos of having a new baby, a new house, and a crazy schedule, it was hard enough to remember to brush my teeth, let alone remember to take the pill. I had a housekeeper, but no nanny, and still managed to take care of the empire we had built.

I was afraid that the negativity surrounding my pregnancy would affect the baby in its early stages. So I called everyone I loved and told them the good news. My family was thrilled, and I quickly began to feel better about the pregnancy. Ah, some positive vibes were just what the doctor—rather, the ob-gyn—ordered.

During my second pregnancy, Terry was cast in the starring role of another movie called *Suburban Commando,* to be shot on location in Los Angeles. My hometown! We made plans to move to L.A. for a few months, which I was really excited about. There's nothing like going back home and being close to my family, especially with a baby daughter and another child on the way. I had spent so many years on the road with Terry, living in Minnesota, Connecticut, and Florida. This was a much-needed homecoming for me.

We quickly set up shop on the West Coast. My parents let us

rent a house from them that they had recently bought for spec. No first or last month's rent. No security deposit. Just move right in! Of course, we paid them some rent, but not much. My mother helped furnish the house and got it completely ready for us, since I was pregnant and really couldn't do much to help. I also found a new doctor in L.A. who would deliver the baby.

Thankfully, I was not as big during this pregnancy as I was with Brooke. There were some complications though. The baby was lying sideways and deep in my body. He was positioned in my uterus in such a way that the circulation on the whole right side of my body from my vag on down was cut off. I had really bad varicose veins in my right leg. My leg was throbbing and felt like it was on fire for almost the entire nine months.

Terry started filming the movie and we settled into our new schedule. He found a Gold's Gym near our rental home and started training. Once in a while, I rallied and went to the gym with him. Since I was pregnant, I did what little exercise I could do. Working out together was more of a way to spend some time together than anything else.

While at the gym a woman approached me and mentioned how much she liked my hairstyle. I was wearing it in two braided pigtails just like I always did. The woman's name was Cory Everson, a professional bodybuilder who won Ms. Olympia six times. Her figure was absolutely flawless—lean and tan with sexy muscles. She would end up becoming better friends with Terry than with me because he was at the gym every day. I was eight months' pregnant and it was more difficult the second time.

A week or two later, Terry told me that he was going to start training at another gym—which Cory and her husband, Jeff, went to—that had more weights. Cory was married, so I didn't mind her hanging out with Terry. However, I didn't know that her husband traveled a lot for business. Terry would get up early and go to the gym near her home and train. The workouts become longer and longer and more frequent—every day, in fact. Then, his workouts went from lasting two hours to four hours.

One afternoon, Terry and I were supposed to have lunch together after his workout. I hadn't gone out that much since I was pregnant, so I got all dressed up. I waited for him to pick me up, but he was late. Thirty minutes went by. Then an hour. (There were no cell phones back then, so I just waited.) *How could he forget?* I wondered. Terry finally came home two hours late. He claimed that he was late because he wasn't familiar with where the gym equipment was located.

I got that sinking feeling that maybe he was doing a little more than working out with the machines. I began to think that he might be having an affair. His long workouts and crappy treatment of me left me wondering. The fact that they had so much in common with bodybuilding made me feel like an outsider. I had read that if a man has his first affair, it's usually when his wife is pregnant. Here's why:

- The husband becomes jealous because he is not being shown the attention he was shown before.
- The husband wasn't really ready to have a child and shows anger toward the wife for getting pregnant.
- The wife may not want to have sex during pregnancy because her body is changing—she has

morning sickness and sensitive breasts and is tired
and emotional.

- A husband can't deal with the hormonal ups and
downs (aka mood swings) that his wife is experiencing during pregnancy.
- Pregnant women can't drink and party, so instead
of the husband staying home with you and making
it a Blockbuster night, he hits the bars and clubs
with his friends.
- While you and your husband are wandering
around the mall shopping for maternity clothes,
you notice that he has a wandering eye and is
checking out newer, slimmer models.

ON JULY 26, 1990, TWO WEEKS BEFORE MY DUE DATE, I BEGAN TO
have contractions. My mom checked me into the hospital, and
Terry arrived soon after. Brooke's delivery was late, but this baby
was early. You just never know. I went into the delivery room
bright and early the next morning at 7:30 A.M., they prepped
me, and at 8:10 A.M.—the same time that Brooke was born—I
delivered an eight-pound, seven-ounce boy. He had white-blond
hair, soft pink skin, and the cutest face ever. It was such a joyous
occasion that I seemed to forget any anger I had toward Terry. I
just held our child closely and cried with joy.

Our new baby was so small in size compared to Brooke at
birth. I thought of lots of boys' names, but none of them seemed
to suit him. For three days I held Mr. No Name in my arms,
looking down at his turned-up nose, rosebud mouth, and perfect

little body and wondering what to call him. Then my mom suggested Nick. I immediately liked it. Terry agreed. Nick was it! Enter stage left: Nicolas Allen Bollea.

Nicky was always such a sweet angel. Brooke was so smart and ahead of herself, but Nick was exactly his age. He was younger, weaker, and smaller. He had twenty thousand ear infections as a baby, and I gave him the back-to-back pink medicine every week. I just had to take extra care of him. But even at that age, he was a man's man. Terry realized that he wasn't just a crying mouth to feed, but a soft, sweet baby, a good boy, and his little man. Terry cared for him deeply. And Nick and I have that special mother-son bond. Nick was always sensitive, not a roughhouse type. He has never spoken a harsh word about anyone and has never talked back or raised his voice to me. As an adult, I'm sure he has dealt with the pressure of being compared to his father. But there's only one Hulk Hogan—and Nick has always respected his father. Nick had his own dreams and never felt that he was supposed to fill his dad's shoes.

When I brought Nick home from the hospital, things were good for the first two weeks until Brutus, Terry's wrestling buddy and party animal extraordinaire, moved in with us in California. He was recovering from surgery after a parasailing accident. When the accident happened, it was pretty scary because Brutus almost died. Terry felt better knowing that his friend was in his house getting the best care possible. I have always been the nurturing type, so as Brutus recovered in the bed upstairs I brought him breakfast, lunch, and dinner. With two babies also under the same roof, I had my hands full. Brutus had broken bones throughout his face and his jaw was wired shut, which meant I had to cook a soft diet for him. Not to mention, I cooked a protein-packed diet for Hulk. It was Mickey Mouse pancakes for Brooke and formula for Nick.

At the end of the day after taking care of everybody, I was wiped out. I certainly didn't feel like having sex or initiating it. I think Terry knew not to bug me. It ran through my mind that maybe he was getting sex somewhere else. To me, there was no excuse to go outside of our marriage. I don't think he realized what I was really going through on my end taking care of two kids and his friend. I was putting myself out there for Terry, and I didn't feel like I was getting anything back from him emotionally or physically.

When Nick stopped nursing, I got a nanny to watch the kids while I went to the gym to work out and try to get my bod back in shape. I thought it would be okay if I left the house for just an hour or so to do something for myself. I mean, how much can one really take of cleaning drooling faces, changing bandages, and washing dishes? And then there were the kids! When I told Terry that I wanted to work out with him again, I was shocked when he said that he didn't want to go to the same gym together. He told me that he liked the gym equipment better at another gym, which was the same gym where Cory trained. As I mentioned, the workouts had become longer and longer. Between the workouts and his film schedule, I wouldn't see him till the wee hours of the next morning! Something was wrong with that picture, and I had that uneasy feeling again that something was going on between them. Although I was scared of Terry's reaction, I did accuse him of sleeping with Cory. Terry denied it and went on to make me feel like a crazy, hormonal, insecure wife. I had two young children and I wanted to think the best. I wanted to believe him. So I made excuses for the entire situation. He always made me doubt myself, and I eventually started believing him. *Yeah, I must be crazy,* I thought. *I'm okay looking, a good mom, wife, homemaker. I would have liked to have had exciting sex with him. What's wrong with me? Why am I so angry and doubtful? Besides he's a guy who has it all. Why would he ever want to screw it up?*

Truth is, I wasn't insecure. I was aware. This scenario would go on for years. Eventually, I began reading about how to be a better wife, and then realized I already was a good wife! I turned to books about how *not* to be a victim, how men love bitches, and I tried not to be a pushover—yearning to keep his respect. And then I read books about infidelity, just wondering, what *are* the signs? How can I really tell? It was so hard, but I slowly started to pay more attention to details, how I was feeling, and how he was acting.

Terry was busy filming *Suburban Commando,* so he was gone all day and wouldn't return home until very late at night. I never really knew exactly where Terry was or who he was with the majority of the time.

When Terry's workouts with Cory hit the four-hour mark every day, the anger began to mount. It really bugged me, and I was at the end of my rope. Was I paranoid? Insecure? Or was my husband having an affair? I needed to put my mind at ease and make sure that Terry was a man of his word. So I hired a private investigator. Honestly, I was disappointed that I had to take this measure and equally scared that Terry might find out. If he ever did, I knew that he could react violently because he was taking a lot of steroids and a never-ending flow of pain pills. Remember, these are hormones that create highs and lows like you could never imagine. I never knew what mood Terry would be in or what I would have to contend with on a daily basis. Ironic, but *he* was the hormonal one!

The investigator posed as a gym member and watched Terry and Cory work out for three days straight. What he witnessed was the two of them training, but mostly touching and Cory rubbing Terry's shoulders and neck as he sat on one of the machines in between sets. After their workout, Terry got in her car and they drove to her house. They went inside together for about thirty to forty-five minutes. Then they came outside and drove back to the gym in her car. They parted ways with a kiss good-bye in the parking lot, and both drove off.

Later I asked Terry where he had been. He said he and Cory had a bite to eat and then he stopped at the vitamin store. That might have been true, but why didn't he mention stopping over at Cory's house and riding in her car with her?

The investigator said he couldn't follow them inside of her house, so he didn't actually have proof of a sexual encounter. But, in his experience, he said that from how they acted and the body language they displayed that my husband was probably having an affair. That was all I needed to hear.

Hearing the investigator say they were probably having an affair sickened me. I remember saying to Terry, "Why do you have to keep training with Cory?" I wonder if Cory's now-ex-husband ever realized how much time they spent together.

I didn't know what to think. The last thing that you want to believe is that your husband is fucking around on you. If I really had known for a fact that he was having an affair with Cory, I would have left him. But that little strain of uncertainty kept me wondering and I stayed. It puts that element of the unknown in your lap. Then you're faced with having to deal with looking at yourself in the mirror. *What the fuck is really happening here, Linda?* I asked myself, confused as hell. *Look in the mirror. What is going on? Listen to your little voice. Listen to your heart of hearts.*

On the one hand, I didn't want to sit there and imagine something that wasn't there. On the other hand, I didn't want to lie down and have someone run over me. I didn't know which direction to go in. It was truly confusing.

Because I didn't have proof that something was going on, my mother and my family said that I didn't really know for sure if he was cheating. They felt I needed to make my marriage work. I had two babies and what was I going to do? Where was I going to go? What would the kids think of me later in life if I pulled them away from their dad? I didn't want my emotions to get the best of me. When I looked at the situation, leaving was overwhelming. I took the path of least resistance. I really never knew if he had the affair. I still don't know, but I will always have that intuition.

Innocent until proven guilty, I guess.

Chapter Six

THE OTHER WOMAN

IVING IN CALIFORNIA WHILE TERRY FILMED HIS movie ended up being miserable! As soon as Brutus was feeling better and had recovered from his injuries, Terry started taking him to the movie set. The party was back on. All of a sudden two female assistants from the film crew were coming to the house every morning and the four of them all rode in the limo that the film company sent for Terry every day. I feel Brutus always set a bad example for Terry. He was a party animal and a risk taker. He's one of those guys who probably should be dead by now. He was still single and whenever they hung out, they always ended up in a strip club.

With Terry now a father of two, I didn't like him hanging out with Brutus any longer. Brutus always had a new stripper on his arm in every city. *What's Terry doing with him when they're out of town?* I wondered. *Does Terry have a stripper, too?* Since I had a new life that centered around the children, I couldn't go to every city anymore. Now my suspicions shifted from Cory Everson to the two female assistants on the film set. It was always a constant worry, and I got tired of second-guessing everything. *Why would he have those girls riding to the set with him and Brutus instead of meeting them there?* I wondered. *That certainly didn't seem like standard procedure.* Let me tell you, it makes it hard to go about your day when you have that constant mind fuck going on. It hurt me that Terry never considered how it would feel if the shoe were on the other foot! But I do know it made me feel like an ass when I showed up on the set with the children.

In the background, I had my mom, who had been married forever, always telling me to stick through it and not leave. She always found a way for me to forgive Terry and make amends for his actions, blaming it on the stress of his career. My parents understood that Terry had a high-pressure job and was in the public eye. Although they didn't think he was so great before we were married, they were now very proud that I was married to somebody so famous. They liked seeing the money roll in and me living well. But they weren't fully aware of what went on behind the scenes.

My mom and dad weren't about to tell me to just divorce him. If you're a good friend and care about somebody who is having problems in their marriage, you're probably going to tell them to work through it. Ironically, my father as a policeman often had the same pissed-off attitude that Terry had when he came home from work. My mother taught me that you don't want to anger them further because it will only make matters worse. Let them get a good night's sleep and when you both wake up the next morning, start fresh. That mind-set encouraged me to continue to be the bigger person in our marriage. I tried to make every day a new day. Who knows if it was the right or wrong advice back then? I just accepted it because I couldn't make a decision for myself at that point. I had to focus on the big picture. Allowing myself to doubt every little flaw would have made me crazy. I didn't want to constantly barrage Terry with questions about every detail of his trip or about who was on the phone. I didn't want him to see me as an insecure, nagging wife. I wanted him to think he had to keep up with me!

Once Terry wrapped the movie in California, I was actually happy to go back home to Florida. Terry was training at his own gym again, and I was more at ease. It was time to just put all of those accusations and negative thoughts behind us. After spending so many Christmases with Terry on the road, now that we were all home together as a family I wanted to try to make the holidays special.

IN DECEMBER 1996, SANTA'S WORKSHOP IN FLORIDA WAS WORKING overtime! I was the busy little elf, wrapping gifts for the kids as well as shipping presents off to my family in California and Terry's business associates, other friends, and family. Santa Hogan's list of people to buy for—whether they were naughty or nice—was always huge, and it took a lot of planning and shopping by me. You can't simply shop for those big wrestlers at Lord & Taylor's. Not to mention, dressing up the house and planning our Christmas party. I decorated the tree with beautiful ornaments and enough lights to guide Santa's sleigh. I also put up a separate tree for the kids filled with all the ornaments they made in school over the years. I enjoyed making it nice.

I always tried my best to make each holiday over the top because that was how it was for me growing up. Lots of food and fun! On the other hand, Terry never had elaborate Christmases during his childhood. Holiday traditions for him were on a much smaller scale because his family had struggled financially during the better part of his early life. His mother and father had a small home, and each year they would take out a tiny artificial Christmas tree from their closet and place it on the coffee table. It had a few little lights and ornaments and would be put away fully decorated for the next year. Terry wouldn't receive much for Christmas when he was a kid, and I loved doing Christmas big because he loved it as much as the kids.

I know Terry's parents were very poor and tried to do their best. That's why I felt that part of my role as his wife was to show him how to celebrate Christmas. Terry had a chance to do it all over again and create holiday traditions with his own family. I even got him into singing Christmas carols around the piano, and, of course, Brooke the little singer led the way!

Right before the kids would go to sleep, I had Terry put on a Santa Claus outfit. Then I told him to go outside on the balcony and make noise to surprise the kids. I'd round up the kids and get their attention by calling out, "Look! Santa Claus is here!" Brooke and Nick were only six and eight years old, so it was huge for them. They'd run to the window and yell, "It's Santa!" Then I'd take them back inside so Terry could sneak back in, change back into his robe, and join in all the excitement. Creating imaginary stuff for the kids to believe in was just as much fun for Terry and me as it was for them.

WITH ENORMOUS FAN RECOGNITION AND CONSTANT VISIBILITY, Terry continued to branch out into new marketing and licensing deals. People would ask him, "Don't you get tired of all the fans bothering you?" Terry would respond, "No, I would get tired if they *stopped* bothering me."

Back in 1994, Terry had inked a deal to be the face of a franchise of restaurants called Pastamania. The family restaurant chain was to open in shopping malls across the country, with the first being at the biggest—the Mall of America in Bloomington, Minnesota.

Terry and I used to live in Minnesota when we were first married, so he was treated like a king in Bloomington. We flew there with the kids for the grand opening party, which was sort of a homecoming for us. We met with all of the executives and employees who were there working really hard to bring this project to fruition. The event was held in a banquet room at one of the city's top hotels. Everywhere you turned you saw Hulk Hogan's face: banners, posters, and T-shirts. Even cookies had his image on them. Our kids loved eating them, turning to me giggling and saying, "Look, I ate Daddy's head."

I was sitting alone near the snack table holding Nick while Terry made the rounds shaking hands, with Brooke proudly standing by his side the whole time. She's always been Daddy's little girl! While Terry continued his meet and greet, I noticed an older dark-haired woman standing nearby staring at me. Being the wife of Hulk Hogan I was used to people staring, but this seemed different to me. I shot a soft smile her way, hoping to break the awkward staring contest. It must have worked because the woman came over and introduced herself. Her name was Kate Kennedy, and she was the public relations person for Pastamania. Kennedy seemed overly interested in my personal life, asking a lot of questions, almost as if *she* was writing a book. How old are the kids? Where are you from? Where do you live? What is it like being married to the Hulk? She even asked about the construction of our new home. I was nice and tried to answer her, but I really felt she was getting too chummy and personal. After twenty minutes of being interviewed by her, I decided to politely excuse myself and end the conversation. *Why was she asking so many questions about Terry and me?* I wondered. I just chalked it up to her being excited to meet us since she was working on the Pastamania project, but I didn't realize she would come back to wreak havoc on our lives a few years later. At the time, I was just happy that the opening seemed like a big success.

A FEW DAYS BEFORE CHRISTMAS, THE DOORBELL RANG AT OUR home on Saint Andrews Drive in Florida. "I'll get it," I called out to our housekeeper, Patty (who had been with me since Brooke was four months old). I opened the door, and from the serious look on the man's face in front of me I didn't think he was a Christmas caroler. He was holding an envelope and asked if

I was Terry Bollea. "No, that's my husband," I said. "He's not here. Is there something I can give to him?" He refused and said he'd be back another time.

While it seemed a bit strange that he wouldn't leave the envelope with me, I didn't have much time to ponder it. Patty and I were busy preparing for my family's arrival from California to spend the holidays with us. I was thrilled to finally have Christmas with my entire family present—the only present I really wanted. The man returned two more times, but Terry still wasn't home. I started to wonder why he couldn't give the envelope to me. What was I *not* supposed to know?

Well, the same deliveryman came back the day before Christmas with that same envelope. Terry had just gotten home from a road trip and answered the door himself. As the deliveryman drove away, I watched Terry from afar step outside onto the porch, open the envelope, read the letter, and put it back inside. He squeezed his forehead, came into the house, and immediately headed up to our bedroom. *Why is Terry so upset?* I wondered. *What's this all about?* I had a lot of questions, and I wanted to know what it was about, but since Terry didn't mention the paperwork—he always had a ton of contracts, agreements, and so on to look at—I decided not to either. I made the best of things and pushed forward with lots of holiday spirit. That night we left cookies and milk out for good ol' Saint Nick, put the presents under the tree, and stuffed the stockings after the children went to bed. All the while, Terry was clearly not present mentally. We went to bed and didn't have sex that night. I just assumed he was exhausted. Then again, setting up Christmas had taken its toll on me, too. I am one of those women who do too much. I'm like a camel: just load me up. I always try to accommodate everybody and everything. I hate telling people no. Linda was always the last person on my priority list. I would end up making excuses for two more decades, always thinking about my own needs last.

I didn't sleep well that night. My head was spinning. Could Terry be cheating on me? Is that why he was acting like this? If Terry was having an affair, he was still very concerned about keeping his marriage together. With all of his sneaking around and making excuses and with me at home with the kids, I really had no idea what was going on with him on the road. Of course, his friends always acted as his liaisons. And then there were the excuses I made. Since he was world famous, I thought for sure that if he cheated, it would be in the newspaper or in a magazine or that it would get back to me somehow. However, the truth was that not a lot of people in the general public knew the Hulkster was married or had children. In those days, there were maybe two tabloid magazines and no camera phones or Internet. Today, there are countless gossip magazines and websites, and, of course, TMZ and Radar Online.

When Terry did come home from the road, he always wanted sex the first day he was back. He liked me to give him oral. Or he liked to have quick sex. It was never an emotional lovey-dovey lovemaking session with candles and cuddling. No, it was more or less a quick fuck. *As long as he's happy and satisfied,* I thought. I never thought there should be a side to sex that would make me happy, too. I just felt great that I was able to make him feel so great. But I remembered when Terry came home from the trip to Minnesota when he was inking the deal with the Mall of America, he went straight up to the bathroom and locked the door. He was edgy and cantankerous. He was not affectionate in the least. I could obviously tell he had something bigger on his mind, but I didn't know what it was. Terry just made me think it was business and par for the course with wrestling. I had no idea what was really going on, so I just tried to stay out of his way. I tried not to think about the *what-ifs*, but since then I was always suspicious that something had happened back in Minnesota. I just had no proof and wanted to think positively. It was Christmas after all!

Christmas morning arrived and the kids were up bright and early. We all drank coffee as we watched Brooke and Nick rip into their gifts. All the while, Terry seemed out of it, distracted. He also appeared to be nervous around my parents.

After cleaning up the wrapping paper, my mom and I got busy in the kitchen preparing Christmas dinner. While the food was cooking, I went upstairs with Terry to take a twenty-minute nap. Christmas was exhausting! I tried to cuddle with him, but Terry was removed and distant—his mood becoming heavier than the eggnog. I kept thinking it was Terry being exhausted or nervous about my parents being there. He was removed mentally and emotionally, again just going through the motions.

THE NEXT MORNING, IT WAS MORE OF THE SAME. TERRY CAME home from the gym in a nasty mood and said he needed his space. I had had enough of his behavior. We began to argue and my mother intervened, trying to calm Terry down. It proved to be a mistake. He snapped, yelling back at her impatiently. He said he was sick of all of the bullshit and ordered my parents to leave.

Terry was a very scary sight when he was mad! My dad stayed quiet as he watched my mom pack their belongings into their suitcases. I couldn't believe this. Terry just threw my parents out of my own home! My folks walked out the front door with no ride and me crying in the driveway, begging them not to go. They thought it was best if they headed home. A taxi arrived soon after, and just like that, Christmas was over.

For the life of me, I didn't understand Terry's anger, rage, and coldness. He took things too far. I stood in front of him demanding an answer. "What's going on? What's your problem?" I yelled. He had ruined the beautiful Christmas for all of us.

"You're the problem," he shot back. "You make me sick."

He told me to sit down on the sofa in his office and listen to him. He told me not to move. I was scared of him because it was clear he was in a rage. Whether he was my husband or not, a three-hundred-twenty-five-pound wrestler is intimidating. He lit a big fat cigar and blew the smoke directly in my face for the next twenty minutes. I don't remember what he was saying. I only recall trying to get up and him pushing me back down onto the sofa, blowing more smoke in my face and his eyes burning a hole in me. I would learn later that he was really just mad at himself, but taking it out on me. Control and losing control are equally bad. A little bit goes a long way.

This type of behavior wasn't rare. He had had outbursts like this in the past, and they were always scary. A steroid rage? Pain pills wearing off? A bad phone call? The kids acting up? Something I said? I never knew what would set him off, but it always seemed to be my fault. Once again, he was controlling me with his moods.

Nick woke up from his nap and began to cry. I begged Terry

to let me check on Nick, but he refused. Nick cried for ten more minutes and Terry wouldn't let me go to him. All of a sudden, Terry's spell broke and he said, "Go get the kid and get out of my face." I escaped, crying, my mind racing about what to do.

I got the children, put them into the minivan, and took off crying. I was afraid to go back home, but where could I go with two small kids? Then, a few hours later it was getting dark so I drove back to the house. Thank God his car wasn't there. It was such a relief. Terry came in later that night as I pretended to be asleep, afraid of another confrontation. He never came to bed that night. I don't know where he slept, but it wasn't with me.

That next morning, Terry left for the gym before I awoke. I was making the kids breakfast when I heard the front door open. As I made the eggs I stayed quiet.

He entered the kitchen, leaned over, and kissed me. I was relieved that he wasn't angry anymore. His new mood surprised me. He showered, came downstairs, and told me that we needed to talk.

"Okay, let's go outside," I said.

"No, let's go to the beach house," he suggested.

Terry asked Patty to watch the kids. The ride to the beach house was dead quiet in his Mercedes. We drove there fast, but it wasn't as quick as the thoughts rushing through my head. *What does he have to talk to me about?* I wondered. *What could make him so nasty to me? What could it be that is so important he needs to tell me about it at the beach house? Was it about our future? Was he going to tell me that he doesn't love me? Does he want a divorce? Were those medical papers? Does he have cancer? Did he get fired? Did someone die?*

I felt sick, weak, and scared. So scared.

Terry sat me down on the sofa at the beach house. This time he sat down right next to me. He began to discuss the turn of events on the road with Pastamania. He asked me if I remembered the dark-haired woman at the opening party. I told him yes. My heart was beating out of my chest, and I realized I could hardly breathe. Then he said that one night when he was in Minnesota, he went to his hotel room and the PR woman stopped by late at night with T-shirts to be presigned for the opening.

My heart was sick. I felt like I was in the Twilight Zone. I was speechless. I began crying and asking questions, trying to put the puzzle together in my mind. Terry was a married man, and you don't just let a strange woman into your hotel room. Terry swore up and down that he did not sleep with her, but what he did admit doing was more than enough: he cheated on me, and this time it definitely wasn't my imagination.

What was he thinking? Where was I? Did he call me that night? Did he wear his wedding ring? Did she know he was married? Who knew? The lies. The fights. The omissions of truth. Terry telling me that I was crazy all of the time. I felt like an ass.

My head reeled as I sat next to him on the sofa. He told me that he needed my support. All I could think about was all the women I had suspected he was with in the past.

Terry was an icon to children all over the world. There were billions of dollars involved with licensing and merchandising agreements. What would the public think of their hero now? After all, his motto was "Train, take your vitamins, and say your prayers."

Terry was repenting, saying over and over again, "I really love you. I don't want to ruin our family."

He gave me every excuse in the book to get me to stay. I definitely held the cards.

I probably had more power than I thought during our marriage. It was just a situation where he was the kingpin in wrestling and our home. Our lives revolved around him—his job and his schedule. I thought I could get over it and be grateful that he was honest with me. That night in bed my mind started to turn as I began to put the pieces together. I wanted to make this thing go away and sweep it under the carpet, but I definitely had a few more questions that needed to be answered first. I was crushed. I was mad. I was scared, and I wanted to leave him.

The next morning I read him his rights, so to speak. "I hope you appreciate that I am staying married to you and not disrupting our family, because your whole world would cave in if I left."

I was so mad that he could put our family in this situation, and I still had so many unanswered questions, which only fueled my suspicions. Terry expected me to just go on, sing songs with the kids and make them more peanut butter and jelly sandwiches. But I was totally distraught. I felt like an empty shell, when he was the one who should have felt that way. My marriage was never the same after that. I felt like a hostage, afraid to do what my heart and my head wanted to do. I wanted to leave him, but I was too scared and too alone.

I told Terry I needed to go back home for a bit. I explained that I was not going to leave him or file for divorce. I just needed some time alone. He understood and was okay with it. I left for California the next day.

Picking Up the Pieces

There was so much I didn't know about what had happened with Kate Kennedy, so much that Terry wouldn't tell me. Terry said things had to be kept hush-hush and only discussed with the lawyers. I understood that things needed to be kept quiet, but I wondered if I could ever trust my husband again. And without trust, how strong can a marriage really be? I just wish Terry would've told me the complete truth back then. I felt sure that I knew only part of the story. Terry told me that the legal problem regarding Kate Kennedy's charges had been going on behind the scenes for a while with the lawyers, and he almost had this problem "put to bed." Interesting choice of words.

Macho Man was in Minnesota with Terry and Kate Kennedy when all of this was going on between them. Here he was coming over to the house all that time, with me making dinner for him, and I knew nothing about what was happening.

I had a wood table in the house that Brooke had made a big ding in when she was a baby. I eventually let her carve her name next to it. Then it became what we called the "autograph table," and visitors would carve their name into it. I remember one night when Terry and Macho Man drank six bottles of red wine and Macho Man carved into the table "Whatever it takes." I never knew what that meant back then. I feel now that it had to do with the affair and interpret it as meaning, no matter how much you had to lie, how much money you had to pay . . . whatever it takes, brotha. Real macho, right? His other catchphrase was "I'm not talking." I assumed it was interview lingo for their wrestling angles!

I was faced with a big decision. I could leave with my two kids and be in the right to do so. Or I could stay with Terry and try to love and trust him again. If I decided to stay, I honestly didn't know how I was going to be a devoted wife again. I felt immense pressure to muster up the strength to find love and forgiveness in my heart. When I was angry, I told Terry that I felt like taking the kids, moving to Hawaii, and never seeing him again. And I meant it. But, given the circumstances, he needed my help because he was in a world of shit. He had a lot riding on his good name and image. Terry apologized, held me, and begged me to stay. He needed his wife to stand strongly by his side, and that's what I did. But I lived in my own private hell, not being able to talk to anyone about it, afraid to ask a lawyer for advice for fear Terry would find out. I put on my happy face for everyone when the truth is I just wanted to cry without stopping.

Terry was trying hard to show me that he regretted what was happening. He changed his phone number. He went back to doing the little things like making me coffee in the morning and taking the kids to school. He even bought me a new car and jewelry. Guilt gifts! His tail was between his legs, and he was totally submissive. And he needed to be. He needed to be sorry and show that he was sorry. Terry wanted it to all to be water under the bridge, but I felt like I was drowning.

I knew I needed to offer him forgiveness, but it was tough. Sometimes I would wake up in the morning and I'd be making the kids breakfast, and he would walk downstairs nonchalantly and act as if everything was normal again. He expected me to make him breakfast, too, like old times. I would look at him and smile, make his breakfast, and act normal, but truthfully I didn't give a shit if he starved to death. I was still so angry.

It took months to heal. I felt betrayed, ugly, empty, angry, and embarrassed. I didn't want his penis inside of me. I didn't trust him anymore. I didn't care if I looked pretty. I didn't care if he was okay, or if he was happy or sad. I hated myself now, and I hated him even more for doing this to me. To us. To our family. The trust was *gone*.

I hadn't said anything, but I called my mom and dad for advice. I had to tell my folks. They reminded me that he was still the father of our children and that maybe I should give him a second chance. He seemed like he was genuinely sorry, still loved me, and wanted to make things right. If I decided to leave, they pointed out, life might not be better on the other side of the fence, mainly for our kids. My family encouraged me to work through this and try to be the bigger person—to take one for the team. Reluctantly, I tried.

I was married to Hulk Hogan. He was a superstar, and the outside pressure from people—the business, the fans, our friends—was undoubtedly immense. It wasn't an excuse, but taking a moment to think about it made me realize that if the public knew the truth, it would be a domino effect: the crumbling of an empire. Plus, my kids were so young and innocent. I had to stay.

I realized that if I told Terry that I forgave him I needed to show it. I wanted no part in doing back to him what he had done to me. It would just put me in the same category he was in: the gutter! Instead, I got busy with life and moved on from the incident as best I could. I put all of my feelings out there knowing I could get hurt again. I gave Terry 100 percent of whatever I had left. It was day by day, minute by minute. I had relapses of anger, questions, and fears from having such low self-esteem, but I moved on.

I never really knew the real circumstances surrounding the Kate Kennedy accusations and Terry certainly wasn't telling me the whole truth. From what I gathered, Kennedy had filed a claim for sexual battery and Terry needed to fight these charges in court and in the media. Unless I stood proudly beside him, he would lose both battles. He might as well have been a politician, because I was playing the politician's wife. Who knows how many hundreds of thousands of dollars we spent on attorney fees getting Terry out of that mess? A confidentiality agreement was entered into. How could he do this to us?

I wondered if Terry really had *wanted* me to stay or if he just really *needed* me to stay.

I was horribly depressed. I felt so lonely. Because he was famous, I couldn't tell anyone about it. If I went to friends or a psychologist, word could get out and it could be the end for him, professionally. I was trapped. It was horrible. Even though I spoke to my family in absolute confidence, they were three thousand miles away. Everybody I had to deal with on a daily basis was in Florida. Not being able to tell anyone how I felt was so difficult. When the housekeeper would show up in the morning with her bright sunny smile, I would begin to cry. I eventually opened up to her. I couldn't hide it anymore.

It took me weeks, if not months, to smile again. It was hard to put on a brave face for my children. They would make cute little jokes and hug me and ask, "What's wrong, Mommy?" The pureness of them and the abrasiveness of my own private life made me just want to cry. I started doubting everything. Every word he said. Every excuse he made. Every place he said he was. Every place he said he was going to go to. Pretty soon my marriage was like a piece of paper with a few pinholes in it. Then the pinholes became tears, shreds, and big gaping holes, and after a while it was just completely torn apart. I had to hold it together, for my family and for my husband's career.

Chapter Seven

GUILTY PLEASURES

ALIFORNIA OR FLORIDA—THAT WAS AN ONGOING debate in our marriage. As much as I missed having my family around and raising our children with my family in their lives, I honored the commitment I made with Terry and we stayed in Florida.

In 1992, we had been searching for a bigger house and finally fell in love with one on Willadel Drive in Belleair. It was an old Spanish-style mansion from the early 1900s, positioned right on the water. Legend has it that the home once belonged to an old mafioso who became extremely wealthy from bootlegging. He had a boat basin right on the property and a seaplane would fly in to drop off the moonshine, which was then sold to the historic hotel nearby. Although it was a magnificent piece of property, the home needed to be remodeled in a big way. The contractors told us that the concrete walls were eighteen inches thick, so the re-modeling would be extremely costly. They suggested bulldozing it and starting over from scratch. Terry and I agreed. The lot cost $2 million and we would embark on spending another $7 million to build our dream home. There was no "dream a little dream" when I was married to Terry . . . we always dreamed big.

Years before, I had seen an unusual house on Lake Arrow-head in California. A wealthy shipping magnate had a chateau in France moved to California, and it was breathtaking. I remember saying to myself that if I ever got a chance to build a home, I would want one like that.

Well, I had my chance.

Terry loved the idea of having his own gym, a boat dock, and a big office, and he pretty much let me do anything I wanted. I made a trip to France along with my mom, Brooke, and an import tile expert from the States named François. We located unique tile and stone from four-hundred-year-old castles that had been demolished. I had the authentic tiles from those structures shipped in a container to Miami and then on a truck to Clear-water. I wanted the house to look like it had been there for two hundred years, with everything authentic and original. It was ac-tually cheaper than buying the reproduction tiles from Chicago, which would not have given me the same antique look. I also got antiques from Paris flea markets and dishes from quaint French towns. I threw myself into the building of the house. I needed something to do for myself to take my mind off the past.

The Willadel estate we were hoping to build took a year of planning and two and a half years of construction. I was at the construction site, checking closely that everything was running smoothly. Every day, I would drop the kids off at school and then go directly to the site. Later, I would pick Brooke and Nick up and bring them to the new house. If they had homework, I'd let them do it in the construction trailer while I oversaw the crew. My presence at the construction site caused a lot of tension between Terry and me. He expected me to be home promptly with the children after school and wanted me to stay there. A nanny would have been a big help, but I liked the kids with me and they liked to be with me. I loved taking care of my kids. At the construction site there were a lot of guys with their shirts off. Big deal! I wasn't looking, nor did I care. Terry was constantly around actresses and beautiful models in his line of work and I just had to deal with that. I'm pretty sure he didn't like it when the shoe—rather, the construction boot—was on the other foot.

When the house was completed, it had everything we needed. A home gym and glass-enclosed spa, not to mention the views as we were right on the water. I absolutely adored the big kitchen and dining room, where I looked forward to having our friends over for dinner.

It was a magnificent French manor house—a one-of-a-kind place that I put my heart and soul into. In the end, we had built the ultimate showplace for the ultimate showman in wrestling. Looking back, I think the house may have been the biggest guilt gift ever.

Terry needed to get knee surgery, so he scheduled time off from work for the first time in years. While recovering in Florida, he took this opportunity to spend more time with the kids. Prior to this, I had done everything for the kids on my own. All of a sudden Terry was at home and eager to try to chip away at

My big Italian family in 1982. (I was taking the photo. The blonde in the middle is my sister.)

With Terry in Oakland, California, on the day he proposed to me.

With Terry on the balcony at the Miramar Sheraton, Santa Monica, California, in 1981. We took the photo with my camera's ten-second self-timer.

On a boat at Brutus "The Barber" Beefcake's first wedding in Clearwater, Florida.

At our wedding on December 18, 1983: Mr. and Mrs. Terry Bollea.

Five months' pregnant with Brooke and loving it!

From our first family photos:
With seven-month-old Brooke
in 1988.

Brooke in her walker with her
coconut-head hairdo.

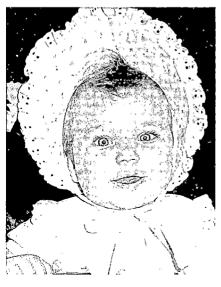

Brooke looking like a little daisy.

Terry and five-month-old Brooke on the beach behind our house in Clearwater, Florida.

Welcoming Brooke's new baby brother, Nick, in 1990.

With Brooke and Nick on the set of Terry's movie *Suburban Commando.*

Terry and Brooke sitting on our staircase after her first day of preschool.

Terry and Nick leaving the hotel in New York for another wrestling event.

Brooke and Nick's first trip to Disney World, Orlando. (Thank God for pop-up strollers!)

Nick posing with Terry after his roller-hockey team won the trophy.

With Terry after we renewed our vows in beautiful Monterey, California.

Terry getting ready to board Hollywood Air, our new private Hawker.

Sitting inside my beautiful new jet with my own custom interior. No more security lines!

My family at a wedding. *Left to right:* my sister, Christie; Aunt Vera; me; my mother; Brooke.

With my dear friend Paige. She's like a sister to me.

Getting ready to give the Hulkster a few surf lessons at my old stomping grounds, Malibu Beach, California.

With Terry in Margaritaville, Key West, Florida.

Partying at the Palms pool in Las Vegas, Nevada.

After I left Terry, Charley was my rock. Here we are as captain and first mate, enjoying the California sunshine.

Charley and me after stopping to admire the beautiful California mountains.

Proud mama bear with my two cubs. Check out the neon nails!

Four of twelve cute, fluffy, lovely dogs!

Like mother like daughter!

some of the duties that were a part of my regular daily schedule. The home had long been my domain, and this took some getting used to; it would be like me jumping into the wrestling ring and being his tag team partner. Quite honestly, at first it was hard having Terry around all the time after he was never home. He was so close to losing us that maybe he realized you don't know what you've got until it's gone!

Although I know Terry adored the kids and loved spending time with them, I also felt he wanted to prove to me after the Kate Kennedy situation that something like that would never happen again in our marriage. He didn't want to just tell me he was sorry, he wanted to show me how he was a changed man and how much he loved me. For my fortieth birthday he bought me a beautiful black convertible Rolls. He got the family our own private jet. Terry bought me a new wedding ring because the stone had fallen out of mine. He also had my name tattooed on his finger. Terry was really trying to make things right with me again and put our life together back in the positive direction it once was. I would have liked to have been more appreciative, but after everything that happened, it was just difficult to be my old self again. It was less about punishing him, and more about staying true to my feelings at the time. He was the one who messed up, and I wasn't going to pretend just for his sake.

Terry wanted to take all of us on a family trip to Carmel, California. We took our private plane to California, picking up my mom, sister, and brother in Los Angeles. We had a couple of really nice days walking around Carmel taking part in wine tastings and enjoying the weather. On Saturday afternoon, my mother told me to get ready because we had a very special dinner to attend. I wore a beautiful blouse with a cream-colored skirt.

A bunch of flowers were delivered to our hotel room, which included a wreath for my head and a corsage. I was baffled. I was curious and didn't understand what was going on. My mom told me, "Terry wants to remarry you." Wow, I felt stupid that I didn't put two and two together. It was our fifteenth wedding anniversary. Again, Terry wanted to make it right with me, and renewing our vows seemed like the next step in reestablishing us as husband and wife. He was clearly pulling out all the stops and not only wanted to apologize privately, but he was doing it publicly in front of my family as well. I appreciated it.

Just like he always stepped up in the ring, he was trying to step up in our marriage.

A Cup of Crazy

Terry enjoyed acting in film and television, but wrestling was in his blood. He loved the sport. He enjoyed the art of the deal. To him, wrestling was his family—his home away from home. Even though it was physically hard on his body, I think he began to miss the wrestling life.

Terry eventually went into business with the World Championship Wrestling organization (WCW), which was owned by Ted Turner. They decided to take the ultimate hero and make him the ultimate villain. Hulk Hogan as a villain? I couldn't imagine it. Hulk Hogan became Hollywood Hulk Hogan. People loved to hate him now but still tuned in to the show.

Terry turning into a bad guy reverberated back into our real life. People would hiss at him in public and they didn't want his autograph anymore. Fans would approach him and say things like, "Why did you turn bad? Our grandson was your biggest fan." Kids would go up to Brooke and Nick at school and ask them, "What happened to your dad? Why is he like that?" Even though Hulk Hogan being a villain was a great business move, I think that it began to bother Terry emotionally. He loved being loved and didn't really like how the fans perceived him now as a bad guy. This new persona was kind of a mental trip for him.

With the success of the WCW, Terry was back again on the road in full swing. It was funny that I had just gotten used to him being around the house all the time, and now he was never home. Terry was on the same hectic schedule as he was in the old days. However, unlike the old days, the kids were older now. I began to feel bored at home alone all day long. I needed a purpose other than taking the kids to school, going to Target, and then picking them up when the bell rang at two thirty. I decided to open my own business, a small used furniture store that offered gourmet coffee and homemade muffins. I named it the French Hen.

I leased an old three-bedroom house that had once been an antique shop. I redid the place and used some of the leftover tile and sinks that were ripped out of our house on Willadel Drive. I filled the store with all of the random antiques I had in my old house and applied for a food and beverage permit. The place was taking shape. Business was booming! The line of customers who wanted to have a cup of gourmet coffee and an oversized muffin while browsing in my little store went out the door. I had a few bistro tables on a patio, and soft music played throughout. Eventually, I installed a full kitchen and offered lunch. I was trying to bring a little twist of L.A. chic to Florida—the type of trendy places you see on Melrose and Robertson boulevards there. And, of course, the food had to be good, too! Florida's cuisine was boring and not the healthiest. It's tough to keep a bikini bod on fried gator and fritter tails, right? I decided to offer some healthier choices for the locals. We served croissants and chicken walnut pineapple salad, among other healthy dishes. Also, there was fresh fruit offered on the plates instead of fries. Everything was freshly baked and prepared. Most of my customers were women, and I did a great lunch business. As the business grew, I was often asked why my restaurant wasn't open for dinner. So a few months later I decided to give it a try at night. Although we did gangbusters for lunch, dinner was not as busy and I eventually ended up closing my little business due to the financial strain. On top of that, I was emotionally drained from what was about to come.

One day when I was working at the restaurant, the manager came into my office and handed over a postcard addressed to me. Written in English, it was from a woman who lived in the Netherlands and said she was a flight attendant. It was not a friendly postcard. This woman wrote a graphic and obscene message that shocked the hell out of me! She wrote that I didn't know her but that she knew my husband and they had been lovers. She wrote that they saw each other whenever they could and even named a date that they were together in Canada. She also wrote that she "loved his cock," among other vulgarities and details about their sexual life. She informed me that she would see him again and there was nothing I could do about it. All this was written in plain view on the back of the postcard.

As soon as I was done reading it, my knees got weak and

I crumpled to the floor. Andrea and Jenny, two of my employ-ees, came to my side. I let them read the card. It was so shock-ing and hurtful after everything I had been through with Terry. I sobbed uncontrollably. It was hard for me to believe that all the time that I was working to reestablish our relationship that this kind of thing was going on behind my back. When I got home, I showed the postcard to Terry. He read it and started laughing. "You really believe this? This is some crazed fan," he said.

Whether I believed him—or I just wanted to believe him—I felt a little better after we had spoken. For the next two years straight, I would receive a postcard a week from this woman. She would continue to tell me where she and Terry hooked up and how she couldn't wait to see him again. She said that they were in love and there was nothing I could do about it and told me how much she disliked me. After close to a hundred postcards, I wondered why they were still coming. I told Terry that I was sick and tired of it. It was embarrassing because the manager of the restaurant handled all the mail at work and I'm sure he read every postcard. The woman talked about things in our house that were dead-on. She talked about events and dates when she met him on the road that were actually right!

Eventually, one day, I was handed a package at the restaurant. I received an audiocassette in the mail from the Cup of Crazy in the Netherlands. I reluctantly pressed Play. The woman told me—in a heavy accent—that she was tired of writing and de-cided to tell me how she felt. She went on to explain that she loved my husband and wanted to be alone with him. She said that he complains about me all the time to her. Then she said that she wanted to cut my face and burn down my house because she didn't like my decorating. She didn't like me being in the way of her relationship with Terry. She ended the tape by saying that she was nine months' pregnant with Terry's child! Oh my God, that was it! I didn't believe Terry anymore. None of it.

My heart was beating hard, and I felt like I couldn't breathe. I was scared. This woman was clearly psychotic and needed to be stopped. I played Terry the tape and told him I was going to hire a private investigator. It was time to get to the bottom of this. I told him that if he was innocent in this situation, then he should come to the investigator with me. Terry told me that he wasn't going to go with me to the investigator, but encouraged me to do so. It angered me that he wouldn't come with me. What was there to hide? Tampa was a small town and Terry had known everyone there since he was young. Word travels fast, and he didn't want to be embarrassed by anything or for rumors to start about trouble at home, especially if they were false rumors.

I found an investigator myself. I took all of the postcards and the tape to my meeting with him. He assured me that he was going to get busy on it and put an end to it. I was relieved. I paid him $2,500 on my Visa card, hoping for someone to help me.

Two weeks went by and I didn't hear anything from him. Then, three weeks. I called the office and the investigator said that he hadn't discovered anything yet. In the meantime, I was still receiving more postcards from the crazy bitch in the Netherlands. I told Terry the investigator hadn't found anything out yet.

I decided to go back to the investigator's office in person, but it was closed down. I found out that he had relocated to north

Tampa. I got his new phone number and told him I was going to drive to his office to pick up the tape and postcards because I was firing him. He said that was going to be hard to do because he lost everything during the move.

I felt my jaw drop. Something was very wrong. It all spelled foul play to me. I can't describe how devastated I felt. I couldn't even drive. I remember stopping in the parking lot of the West Shore Mall in Tampa to try to collect myself. I pulled into a spot and started crying and shaking.

I came home and told Terry that the investigator said he lost all of the tapes and I didn't believe him. I said, "You need to call this guy right now!"

"I'm not calling him," Terry responded.

Terry had been so supportive and encouraging when I first wanted to hire an investigator, but now he didn't want to help me get my stuff back? There was no continuity to his actions or intentions, and my anger knew no bounds. I just felt like I was being fed a line of bullshit. I was so confused. I didn't know fact from fiction. I wanted to believe Terry, so I decided to play investigator myself. I made Terry sit down with me and compare the dates and cities when the woman said she saw him against the dates and cities he had listed in his book. Some of it made sense and some of it didn't. It took me to that insane level where it was hard to look at him or to function. He kept telling me that I was making a big deal out of nothing and that anyone can get his schedule off the TV. It was impossible to look for any clues.

I was working so hard on everything in my life, and now this? I was at my wit's end. Breaking under the stress of my relationship and the pressure of owning a business and being a mom, I decided to close the restaurant. Also, the trust that had been built between Terry and me over the years was extremely fragile. Terry needed to be on his best behavior, and I tried to be tolerant and forgiving. I wanted to be the woman behind the man, but I was questioning everything.

Chapter Eight

GOING THROUGH
THE MOTIONS

URING THE COUPLE OF YEARS LEADING UP TO THE reality show, Terry's career was on a slower track. He was home all the time enjoying being a dad and not having to be on the road 24-7. He loved spending time with the kids and taking Nick to hockey or soccer games. Despite being as famous as he was, Terry would hang out on the sidelines with me and make conversation with the other parents. People were always warm and friendly to him, and he was the same way back. It was nice that my kids had both of their parents cheering them on.

My relationship with Terry at this point was becoming difficult, and it certainly wasn't like a honeymoon. It was more like we were going through the motions. Our sex life was one of convenience for him. And for me, I had so much on my plate with running the household that by the end of the day I was exhausted from taking care of the never-ending flow of people, employees, and friends who were in our home on a daily basis (our housekeeper was part-time, which meant I cleaned up at the end of each day). I would crawl into bed and hit the sheets. I was dead tired, but I looked forward to time alone with my husband to try to reconnect.

Just because I was ready for bed and some snuggling didn't mean Terry was. At eleven P.M. he'd head into his bathroom, turn the TV on, and start his beauty regime of showering and shaving his whole body. It seemed like we could never go to bed at the same time or get on the same schedule. He marched to the beat of his own drum. If Terry could have made some conversation with me or reached over and tenderly touched me and rubbed my shoulders, I probably would have been more responsive to him, but he always seemed so distant.

I was so used to his indifference that I just let it go. I never really spoke up for myself because I didn't want to start a big argument in the middle of the night by saying things like "Shut off the TV. How about having a little conversation?" or "Do you even care what I did today?" If *he* couldn't see that he wasn't paying attention to me, it wasn't worth starting a whole argument about it. I could never win, so I just sort of gave up. Then, he woke me up for sex after I had fallen asleep. Sometimes I just had to get back up and sleepwalk through it. It really confused me why he didn't spend time with me when I was awake waiting for him. I was basically doing my wifely duties. It became unemotional, and we sort of functioned on that level for a while. I tried to keep it as civil as possible, and so did he. We just existed, together but separately. He never seemed like he wanted to talk about his personal feelings. He couldn't look me in the eye. I just needed a little emotion from him but couldn't get it. We became strangers to each other.

I wasn't happy, and I made excuses for my life. *Who exactly out there has a perfect marriage?* I thought. I looked at it and began to rationalize to myself: *I think deep down that my husband really loves me. I know he loves the kids, too. I know that he loves having us there for him.* At that point, I just didn't know how to change anything. Our backs weren't up against the wall enough to where I was ready to either jump or lunge. We were focused on the kids, and that was really what our connection was at that time. I felt like we were still on the mend from his first infidelity, and in spite of everything I still wanted to try to make our family work. I was giving him a second chance!

Brooke and Nick were still going to Saint Cecilia's Catholic School in Clearwater. We had a typical household where I would get up in the morning and make the kids breakfast and pack their lunches. We would race off in the Suburban and drop them off at school. Nick was involved in sports and Brooke was taking piano and singing and dancing lessons. I always tried to have the kids involved in after-school activities. When they came home, we'd do homework together. That was the kind of lifestyle we led.

Because we only had one girl and one boy, each child was treated like an only child. They each had individual love, individual hugs, individual time with us, and many kisses. We had two absolutely beautiful children, and they were raised with morals, values, a conscience, and love. They didn't get everything they wanted, in spite of what most people think. They were good kids. They didn't talk back. They had manners and knew how to behave. We took them everywhere with us—restaurants, airplanes, wrestling events, and red carpets. They were such good kids, so well adjusted and loved by their peers. We were proud of both of them.

We hated the thought of leaving them home with a babysitter or nanny, and I never sent them to camp for the summer because they liked being home with their parents and pets. Life was good.

My relationship with Brooke was wonderful, and it still is. I'm very close with my daughter. Brooke and I are completely open with each other, because I always wanted to be honest with her and prepare her as best I could for all the things that happen in a young woman's life. Growing up, Brooke asked me what it was like the first time having sex. And she asked me about the first time I got my period. I didn't want things to be a surprise to her, so I was always straight up with her about everything (even my disappearing condom story from my teens that I mentioned earlier). I called Brooke "my little girlfriend" from the time she was a baby. She was my bud. Same with my Nick. I love having a son! He has always been such a beam of light in my life. He's always happy and in a good mood. He's respectful of both of his parents. He got extremely good grades and has always been popular and had a lot of friends. When people meet Nick, they instantly love him! He's athletic, good-natured and he's just always been a good kid. Sometimes I would miss my kids so much I would pick them up early from school and we'd go shopping. Or we'd just come home and cook and watch TV.

I had kids to *have* kids. Next thing you know, they start preschool and then they're with teachers all day. They're gone! So I would use all of those sick days and keep them with me. If I could have, I would have had two more kids. I guess that's why I had so many pets.

I'm not going to say pulling them out of school was the best thing to do, but both of my kids were very bright students and levelheaded. I didn't think it would ruin them, especially considering their passions went beyond the traditional school curriculum. Human life experiences are so much more important than having perfect attendance at a school.

BROOKE HAD ALWAYS BEEN THE LITTLE ENTERTAINER AT THE house. It wasn't just Terry, so I guess the apple doesn't fall far from the tree. At two and a half years old, she could barely talk but was already reciting the words to nursery rhymes. She watched *The Little Mermaid* and *The Wizard of Oz* and she could memorize all of the words to those songs, singing them with perfect pitch. At only a few years old, she had a memory like a steel trap and still does. She would make everyone sit on the couch, then come down from her room wearing a twirly dress and perform one of the Disney numbers for all of us. Brooke had a natural ability at the piano as well. I thought it was cute, but I had no idea that it would turn into something that she would want to do for the rest of her life.

When she was fourteen years old, she expressed interest in singing. I was in our pool at our Willadel home floating around on a raft getting some sun when Brooke came outside and slammed the phone book down on the pool deck. "Mom, that's it!" she exclaimed. "I want you to call someone for me because I want to get into acting, modeling, or singing."

I lay there smiling to myself and thinking a simple phone book wouldn't offer the answers. While many parents often try to get their children into acting or modeling, Terry and I never pressured our kids toward any type of career in that direction. But it wasn't us pushing Brooke . . . it was Brooke pushing *us*. It was clear that she was determined and wanted her mother's help.

"It's Sunday and we can't call anybody this afternoon," I said. "Nobody will be at their offices."

"No, Mom," she shot back. "Call anyway because this is something I really have to do."

I got out of the pool and turned to the modeling and talent sections of the phone book. I took a shot in the dark in the bright sunshine and left a few voice mails for people at various agencies. Whether they would return our calls or not, Brooke immediately felt better that I reached out and tried. She's so cute.

Monday rolled around and I actually got some phone calls back. I guess that "Brooke *knew* best" even early on! One call was from an agency in Clearwater that teaches young girls how to do makeup and prepares them for photo shoots. Brooke met with a woman named Diane at the agency and they decided to work together.

Brooke's interest in music quickly took center stage over the acting and modeling. She was inspired by all of the artists I love and listen to from my era: Toni Braxton, Teena Marie, Amy Grant, Carole King, Stevie Wonder, James Taylor, Luther Vandross, and Elton John. She started playing piano with me and also with a piano teacher at an early age. We knew that we had to get the right person involved so she wouldn't lose interest in moving forward as she got older. She began working with a talented piano teacher named Theo who taught her the Alicia Keys and Norah Jones styles of piano and vocals. It was then that I realized Brooke could be the next star in our family.

Lights, Camera, Reaction

It's been said that, "Truth is stranger than fiction." That certainly proved to be the case for our family when we entered the world of reality television.

In 2004, VH1 approached us to do a one-hour special entitled *Hulk Hogan: Stage Dad*. Producers from the Florida-based production company Pink Sneakers came to our Willadel home for a meeting and explained the vibe of the show, which would entail Terry playing "stage dad" and helping Brooke with her music. Brooke was still working with Lou Pearlman in Orlando, and he realized that Brooke had huge potential. She was doing small concerts and actually working with a live band!

They felt this would be a great vehicle to help launch Brooke's singing career as well as put Terry's career back on the map. He was still wrestling now and then, but he had slowed down quite a bit due to hip and knee surgeries. It was probably a bigger draw just to see Hulk Hogan at home.

I think Brooke's singing and dancing background came from

me and her stage presence came from Terry. I would always have music playing in the house, and I sang and played the piano ever since the kids were small. At parties we had, I'd sing karaoke into the mic, and jump up on the coffee table and sing and dance. Brooke and Nick loved my outgoing style and my ability to have fun and not worry what other people thought. I really think that between their dad being a showman on TV and me being one at home, Brooke and Nick loved music and loved people! I took Brooke to lessons and the recording studio. What the heck, if the show would help the kids, then I was on board! We felt that with Terry's recognition, we could help Brooke break into show biz, too. And with her musical ability VH1 was the perfect platform.

Camera crews filmed us for three months straight, mostly following Brooke closely on her career. Once shooting wrapped, our lives returned to just as they had been before. One morning, I was watching the news and the ticker message at the bottom of the screen said that Britney Spears had fired her longtime manager, Larry Rudolph. Although it was a long shot, I thought maybe he could help Brooke launch a career. I called Terry and he felt Rudolph was probably not interested in an unknown. But when I get a gut feeling like that, I fight for it. I knew what I had put into Brooke and what she was capable of doing. And I knew that if Larry Rudolph met Brooke, she could deliver. I had instilled confidence in her, which added to her talent and winning smile. So I had Terry make some calls, to get a hold of Larry Rudolph's office. He returned our call that same day and, surprisingly, he said he would be very interested in helping Brooke. It was an exciting moment for the family and especially for Brooke. They ended up working together for a whole year, and Rudolph was very instrumental in her development as an artist. Things were moving forward in the right direction to record Brooke's first album.

VH1 was extremely pumped up about the footage that was shot for the special. *Hulk Hogan: Stage Dad* aired and resulted in really high ratings. VH1 asked us to continue in our own reality series called *Hogan Knows Best*.

The producers and directors tried to find our unique personalities for the new show based on what we did on a daily basis and what our interests were. Brooke was the aspiring singer and Nick was the typical little brother. He portrayed a modern-day Dennis the Menace, but in a good way. I was a regular June Cleaver—America's mom, but the wife of a celebrity and mother to two kids who were becoming famous in their own right. I wasn't acting my role. I was really just being myself. I was a fun-loving, unpretentious, easygoing wife. I didn't have servants around to wait on us. There was no "Don't touch me I'm in my Chanel suit." Ultimately, it was my own personality that was coming through. First and foremost, I was Terry's wife and a mother.

We didn't know how the behind the scenes of a reality TV show worked. We thought that reality meant that the production crew would be sleeping in our house with us. I was kind of bracing myself for the worst. Then, we realized that the crew people don't stay up for twenty-four-hour shifts. They come over to your house and work an eight- to ten-hour day and follow you around doing whatever happens in your life.

It was a huge learning curve to get used to shooting the show. For instance, we spent the majority of our days walking around with mic packs hooked to our hips. Many times in the early days we'd forget that the mics were still on us and go to the bathroom; the crew would hear us peeing.

The whole family didn't know how the producers were going to put together all of these pieces of footage they were gathering. I really didn't think they were going to feature me very much at all. I had some small scenes at the beginning. For example, I would pop my head in and say, "Brooke, you have a phone call." I expected that. I didn't care. Terry was in it predominately, and then it was Brooke and then Nick and then me. I was fine with that because I was all about Terry and the kids launching and sustaining their careers. I was all about supporting them.

When we saw the first episode edited together with funny music and camera angles, it was just an absolute riot. It was comical to see our family portrayed in a way that made us realize that we were pretty funny! Once we realized how it all worked we wanted to bring more of it! It turned into a very rewarding experience.

I became a creative consultant on the show because the production crew kept looking to me for guidance about what the family was doing, since we were all in different directions. We didn't have wardrobe or makeup people, because Brooke and I had fun doing our own. During Terry's wrestling days, his bright red-and-yellow tights got him way more attention than the wrestlers who wore boring black. The colors grabbed you and made you want to stop switching channels and take in the action. Although these looks didn't work out well in public, they really popped on television. I wanted to do same thing for the visual look of our reality show. In every scene, we wore bright colors like turquoise and yellow, and it made *Hogan Knows Best* a very colorful Florida show. Even though it was kind of goofy, it really worked.

Living in a house where they shoot a television show every day isn't easy. A camera crew of twenty-eight rang our doorbell each morning at eight A.M. During that first season, five major hurricanes ripped through our area of Florida, so we mostly had to shoot indoors. Equipment like additional lights were attached to the beams in the ceiling of our kitchen. We even had a tint on many of our windows to block out the natural light, so it was dark in the house. It was expensive for production to take this stuff down and put it back up every day, so we just lived with it after the cameras left. It was like our house became a set at a television studio. Things were often so surreal that it felt like we were in the movie *The Truman Show*. We started to forget what day it was and what real life was like outside our front door.

It would take two weeks to shoot one episode during season one. After being sandwiched together all day, work was finally over at around eight P.M. Terry, the kids, and I would go out to dinner and then we'd come back home and all go off and do our own thing. Even though we were family and I love my kids more than anything, we definitely needed a break from each other.

We really didn't know the impact the show was going to have until it aired. Fans quickly began to recognize all of us, which was something new for Nick and me. When fans would tell me that I was their favorite TV mom, at first it freaked me out. Moms said they liked me because they could relate to me. Men said they liked me because I was a sexy mom. Teenage girls came up to me because they were excited to meet Brooke and Nick's mom. Prior to this, if I was noticed, it was because I was Hulk Hogan's wife. Now, I was becoming a sort of persona in my own right, just being the wife and mother in the Hogan household. It's heartwarming when you're commended for doing what you love.

Sometimes, men would approach me and say, "I can't believe you're the mom. I thought you and your daughter were sisters." Flattery will get you everywhere! I actually found an old fan letter the other day from a man who wrote that I was beautiful and that Hulk *was* the luckiest man in the world. It made me feel good because, although I felt that my husband might have appreciated me privately, he was always kind of mechanical about it in public. So it was nice when I heard it from a random fan.

Seeing myself all the time on television was a new thing. At first I thought, *Oh my God, I look so fat.* Then I let go of those feelings and stopped being so hard on myself. This was reality television, and the world was seeing me for who I really was. Whether we were shooting part of an episode where I had just woken up in the morning or I was glammed up for a night out with Terry, I was seen at my best and my worst. I didn't feel the need to be skinny to be married to Hulk Hogan or to be the mother of my kids. The public was acknowledging me for what I did as a wife and mother, rather than for how I looked— although I did catch some flak about my wardrobe! I'm just not great at picking out clothes, so I wore whatever I felt like, if it matched my mood. I guess all the years at Catholic school wearing a uniform sort of ruined my ability to figure out "free dress." I always worked out in the gym. But after doing it and watching grams of fat and carbs and living by the scale and mirror, I just got burned out. There is just more to life than a perfect figure!

I believe the public embraced our characters on the show because we weren't afraid to reveal the private side of our lives. Everything was so fun filming as a family. Reality TV was great. The acting started when the cameras *stopped* rolling, and the conversation ended, too.

Extreme Measures

After we shot the first season of *Hogan Knows Best*, a wrap party was definitely in order! The reality was that everyone on our reality show worked their butts off and it was time to let loose and celebrate a job well done.

At around eight P.M. after our last day of shooting, the crew and our family headed over to Shephard's on the beach in Clearwater. About sixty of us had dinner and drinks while a live band played. At about one thirty in the morning Terry wanted to go home, but I wanted to stay for one more dance. The kids were still dancing and having fun with the crew, and so was I.

"Can't we wait to leave?" I asked. "I love this song, and the band is still playing." Terry got more irritated when I insisted on not going home. I didn't want to leave, and neither did the kids. We were all having fun . . . all of us except Terry. I had another drink and continued to get my groove on regardless of his attitude.

When we got home, Terry immediately ripped into me.

"I wanted to leave an hour earlier and you didn't listen to me," he said. "You were partying all night and I was tired. I'm so sick of this crap!"

"What are you sick of?" I asked, confused. "I wasn't dancing with any guys. I was dancing with *your* wrestler friend's wife, Toni! What's your problem?" I replied. "I work full time and do everything for you, and you sat back and glared at me all night!"

"I'm just sick of this," he said, shaking his head. "I can't stand it anymore."

What couldn't he stand anymore? He was the huge partier. Not me. He's the one who talked openly and candidly about his drug and alcohol abuse and pain pill addiction. He was just jealous. I wasn't trying to make him jealous. I just have an open personality and was being friendly and social as I always am. In retrospect, he was probably already setting up to leave me when the show wrapped. I did drink two or three glasses of wine after shooting, out at dinner, but I've never been an out-of-control drunk! When I drank, I'd get happy, laugh, and talk. And if I did lash out after having a couple of glasses of wine, it wasn't because of the wine. I was just sick of the situation I was trapped in, sick of being taunted.

I was forty-five years old, and now Terry picked up the phone and called my mother at two thirty in the morning. "I can't control Linda anymore," he yelled into the phone. "She's out of control and drinking all the time. I'm sick of it. I need your help. I'm sending her home. You deal with her!"

I was shocked at Terry's behavior. Not only did he ruin the fun we were all having at the wrap party, but I was shocked and alarmed that he called my mother three thousand miles away telling her I was basically an out-of-control drunk. I was pissed at Terry for overreacting and scaring my family!

The next morning, he told me he was sending me to California whether I liked it or not. He gave me an ultimatum: check into rehab or don't come back. When I arrived in California, it was like walking into an intervention. Terry had brainwashed my parents into thinking I was an alcoholic without them even hearing my side of the story. My mother scolded me and said she couldn't believe my behavior. She told me that she was driving me, or I was to drive myself, to rehab at the Betty Ford Center.

Terry was Hulk Hogan—Mr. Wonderful to most—and people assumed that his word was *the* word because he was so famous. They were blinded by his star power. The cards were stacked against me. He convinced them that I had a problem and I needed help. If only my family knew what I was really dealing with! I got into my Mercedes and drove to Palm Springs where the Betty Ford Center is located. I was advised by Terry and my family to put in a full month of rehab at the center. *Oh my God,* I thought, *I can't see my kids for a month? I hate him!* How could he lie and do this to me? It felt like a conspiracy!

The next day, I met with a counselor and she asked me a series of questions about my drinking history.

"I don't really have a drinking history," I said. "I do drink two or three glasses of wine with dinner. Other than that, that's about it. I have kids and I'm shooting a television show all day, so there is no time to just sit around and get drunk."

"Two or three glasses of wine?" the counselor asked.

"Yes."

"That's it?"

"Three glasses is my max, because I have to get up in the morning with the kids."

"Tell me about your police record."

"I don't have one."

"Have you ever been arrested?"

"No."

"Have you ever gotten a DUI?"

"No."

"Have you ever blacked out from drinking?"

"No."

"What about prescription medication?"

"I don't take any medication. Sometimes I take Excedrin."

"So you don't take any prescribed medications?"

"No. I don't have any prescriptions for anything!"

"Any dependencies?"

"No, just my kids and my animals."

"Then why are you here?"

"My husband got angry with me because we were out and I had a few drinks. It was a party, and I was dancing and having fun."

"Sounds like your husband is a little jealous."

"Probably," I responded with a sigh. "My father had a drinking problem years ago, and I think that maybe my family thinks I have one, too. But I don't drink in secret or private. I drink in public at a restaurant, or at home with my family and friends."

"I don't think there is any need for you to be here," the counselor stated. "But if you want to stay, you can."

I decided to stay at the Betty Ford Center and prove everyone wrong. I had my blood tested and there wasn't a trace of alcohol or drugs in it. After four days of being in there with people who had AIDS and serious drug and alcohol dependencies, I started to realize this was not the place for me. It was scary, in fact. I had never seen people in such bad shape—blisters on their fingers and lips, with their teeth actually rotting.

After a few more days, I said enough is enough. I didn't want to leave the Betty Ford Center without my parents' permission, but I hated every minute of it and wanted to get out of there. I didn't miss drinking wine. I just missed my children. My mom insisted that Terry decide.

I called Terry from Palm Springs and told him that I wanted to leave rehab early and come back home to Florida. He told me that I could come back as long as I promised to be good and stop drinking for a while. I think he realized how his little plan was turning into a serious life-changing event for not only me but our kids. They missed their mom!

At Betty Ford I had time to think about the state of my marriage. I think the whole reason Terry insisted on sending me to rehab was because he was beginning to lose control over me. For years, I was behind the scenes while Terry basked in the spotlight. I was fine with that. But now I was getting noticed. I wasn't just this girl behind the man, at Terry's beck and call. I was now seen as almost an equal to him, and I think it kind of bugged him. Like I always say, "There is only room for one star at the top." And it was always him. Ironically, I was only doing the television show to help Terry and our children. I never jumped into showbiz before. It wasn't my calling. I liked decorating, fixing up our home, and taking care of our kids and animals. I didn't want to be famous. I didn't need the adoration of anyone except my family and dogs! I loved being a housewife and mom. But now that I was a television personality just like Terry, he kept saying I was out of control.

I wasn't out of control. I just wasn't in *his* control.

One of the ways Terry would control me had to do with the children. Whenever I wanted to put the kids in school in California, he would immediately get on the phone and set Brooke up with a big business deal in Florida. He would always undermine my plans and overpower me with his contacts to continue to keep everything in Florida. Terry would also use the kids against me. If I said red in front of them, he'd say it should be blue. If I said it was okay for Nick to go on a field trip, he would say that it wasn't. It seemed that it didn't even matter whether it was good for the kids or bad for the kids, everything had to go the opposite direction from me. Parents have to always take a unified front when it comes to their kids. He never did that.

Terry would also control me with his moods. He would get into a bad mood for no reason at all, and I would ask him over and over what was wrong. Was it something I did? Something I said? I always felt like I was at fault for his sadness. But this was just another way for him to manipulate and control me. When we would get into an argument, he would often break things that I loved. I had an antique wagon that I used as a bassinet for Brooke and he picked it up and threw it across the room one time. He tore my shirt, threw lamps, and held me down on the bed with his hands around my throat during arguments. Slamming doors. Pounding walls. I was always afraid he would kill me in one of his rages. I started to get fed up with it all, the abuse, the manipulation, which I figured stemmed from his jealousy or something! But what could I do? There was no way to talk it out when he was in a rage like that. So I would usually just get in the car and leave.

I wish I had been more aware of the signs of a controlling husband earlier on. While I'm on the subject, here are some of them:

1. He calls you all day long to keep track of your whereabouts, probably to avoid crossing paths.
2. He knows how to push your buttons and does it often.
3. He embarrasses you in public.
4. He shoves, grabs, and/or pushes you during an argument. You become submissive because you're afraid of triggering another violent rage.
5. He intimidates you by threatening to take away your most precious things, such as your children, pets, homes, and friends.
6. He dictates the rules and tries to control everything in your life—what you do, where you go, what the money is spent on, and so on.
7. You feel like you're being held hostage emotionally, because you're afraid to speak your mind.
8. He convinces you that you can't function and that you're incompetent without him in your life.
9. He never confesses to anything, no matter how much evidence you have. Then he turns the tables saying that *you're* the one who's crazy.

10. He eavesdrops on your conversations and becomes impatient when you're spending time with your friends and family.

When I left Betty Ford, I drove myself back to my house in California. I was by myself and happy to be out of that place. I didn't know if I was going to try to keep my marriage together because I was so bitter and angry at him. I wasn't as angry about him sending me to Betty Ford as I was at the fact that he turned my family and kids against me. I wondered how my husband could do this to my children. Alcoholism? They didn't even know what that was. He scared them into thinking something was wrong with their mom. He even had my own mother believing it, and she wasn't around! I realized he'd had an intervention. Why? Something I never saw coming. Something I didn't understand.

I did think about leaving him at that time. I just didn't know how. That was probably one of the biggest moments of depression that I ever went through. I didn't want to go home, but I missed my kids! I just didn't want to face Terry. I didn't *want* to make it work anymore. I was mad as hell at him. I was mad at my parents for not listening to me. They felt I was out of control at that time. If I had said I wanted a divorce, they would have thought I was spiraling further out of control. I had to regain my self-confidence and my composure. I had to get the control back that was taken away from me so unfairly. I was being bullied in my marriage. I realized at that point I couldn't be the victim anymore.

I really wanted to go back home because my kids needed me. I flew back to Florida just to be with them. They were *so* happy to see me. I can't tell you the joy that filled my body once I held my two kids again. I'll never let anything ever come between me and my kids again.

Terry was glad to see that the kids were so happy. I think he also saw me as defeated and dependent once again. He had finally regained the control he so desperately needed. I remained on my best behavior, all the while being a dumb fox! I knew what he was doing! I also knew in my heart of hearts that I wasn't the one with a dependency problem!

Chapter Nine

WELCOME TO MIAMI

T THIS POINT, *HOGAN KNOWS BEST* WAS THE number one rated TV show in VH1 network history!

We completed season two of *Hogan Knows Best* in Tampa, and our TV ratings were so high that season three was inevitable.

The kids and I were really burned out living in Clearwater. I had taken the kids out of school to make it a little less stressful with the schedule. Filming a hit TV show and still trying to live a normal nine-to-five life outside the walls of our house remained a struggle. Not to mention, from home schooling for the kids to shooting the show every day for two years straight inside the same house, we all felt confined. The situation was taking its toll on us personally. It's pretty tough to imagine that in a seventeen-thousand-square-foot house we were actually experiencing a claustrophobic feeling. Not only were the walls closing in on us, but we were down each other's throats and needed a change.

Ultimately, I felt that if we could have figured out how to bring the show to Los Angeles, it would have been better for Brooke, Nick, *and* Terry. With all of the hype of the television, motion picture, and music biz in Hollywood, I felt it would have improved everybody's career. But Terry liked being in Florida, and it was pretty evident that he was not going to let us all move out to the West Coast. Brooke began to make a push for Miami since she had been going down there so often to record music. We had spent some time in Miami for the VH1 Awards and it seemed like a really fun city. It had a lot more culture and was certainly more in the mainstream than Clearwater. With the music and entertainment industry flourishing in Miami, it was actually quite similar to Los Angeles. I don't think Terry minded moving to Miami because he felt he could do business there. He also had all of his friends there. He was very bent on staying in Florida, so it was a happy middle ground for everybody.

Terry and I looked at houses all over Miami, but there was really nothing to choose from at that time that would suit our needs. We did see one big spec house that could be absolutely fabulous. It had a five-car garage and guesthouses, and the floor plan showed plenty of room for filming as well as fitting Terry's at-home gym. I really thought that this was the answer for us. Plus the kids loved it! Terry liked making them happy.

The huge contemporary house was $12 million and not even

finished yet. It was a cinder-block frame sitting in a pile of mud from all the rain that had inundated Miami the previous winter. I could kind of see what the structure and style of the house was going to eventually become, but it had a long way to go before it was completed, and I had some convincing to do.

Contemporary wasn't my thing as I was more used to antiques and country, but Terry, Brooke, and Nick thought the house was fabulous. We had seen some other houses that the builder had done in the neighborhood that were absolutely stunning, similar in construction but finished. Although nobody else could envision the final look of the house, I could. I knew that I could design an even better home. Spectacular!

We took the leap and bought the house in February 2006 with the promise that the construction work would definitely be completed by May because that was when we were scheduled to start filming season three of *Hogan Knows Best*. The builder swore up and down that he could do it in time. I put my faith in him and ran the job from Clearwater, driving down on weekends to work with the builder on details.

Terry and I decided not to pay for the house in full, but make payments instead. We had enough money in the bank to buy it outright, but we decided to play it safe and see how things went in Miami. Even though we were going to make house payments on this property, I felt strongly that after a year or two, if we wanted to sell the house, we could make a profit.

Miami proved to be good right off the bat for Brooke's career in the music industry. While she was making a personal appearance at Mansion nightclub in Miami, we met record producer Scott Storch. At the time, it seemed like you couldn't put on the radio without hearing one of his collaborations; he'd worked alongside such artists as Nelly Furtado, The Roots, and The Game. Storch loved the music/TV collaboration on our show and was willing to help her out. This was music to our ears!

Storch introduced us to his business partner, who was the head of the record label. After we decided to do business, we all flew down to Miami from Clearwater with cameras in tow to sign the contracts and ink Brooke's deal with her new record producers. They handed her a check and welcomed her to the "family." This was a big event for Brooke in real life as well as for the fans of her music and *Hogan Knows Best*.

Everyone was there from the entertainment company, including the receptionist, Christiane Plante. She sat at the table during the scene we shot for *Hogan Knows Best*. She was built just like me, about five foot seven in height with fair skin and big boobs. She was wearing tight jeans, a white wife-beater, and sexy heels. Christiane had jet-black hair and green eyes. She was in her early thirties and definitely sexy with that body! Little did I know back then that she would eventually prove to be too much of a temptation for my husband.

While the house was being built Terry and Brooke would drive down to Miami for three or four days to work on her music while I stayed with Nick in Clearwater and packed up for the move. We were actually only partially moving because we weren't selling our Willadel home.

I wrote a diary entry on May 10, 2006, that reflected my feelings at the time:

> *We're getting ready for our move to Miami, and it's bittersweet. We were so excited and ready for a change, but*

change is hard emotionally. It's hard to decide which clothes to take or not take. It's hard for me to leave my "home," wishing I was making the move to California instead of settling for Miami. But at this point, any change is welcomed.

Brooke got a record deal and a schedule, which means being gone. Nick has a deal to drive for Dodge, which means a schedule and being gone. I'm missing my two dogs and Lilly the rooster that all died within the last month. We've been confused about what to do for so long and then boom—TV show, moving, selling, full-time work, kids leaving, dogs dying—it's just too much all at once. My house is full of boxes, I'm still not sure of what to pack or not—the new house is so empty. I wish it would just happen or not, but the waiting is putting me on such a bummer because I'm clinging to what is safe and keep changing my mind about the whole thing. In order to stay positive, I need to stay numb emotionally, because when I think about what I'll be missing, it makes me so sad. I should be happy—moving on, fewer pets, less housework, venturing into new territory—but I'm not. I'll just go through the motions—do what I have to do to move, try to stay positive for my family, but I'm just so spent—drained, tired, sad. This is a serious hurdle in my life. What will tomorrow bring?

The day that we left Willadel and headed to Miami, we had our cars loaded on open trucks. As we were heading down Interstate 195 across the Intercoastal, it began raining heavily. All of a sudden, the temperature dropped unexpectedly and the rain turned to hail. By the time we got close to our new house, it was hailing golf-ball-sized pieces of hail. Our beautiful cars were out on this open hauler being pelted. The driver tried to park under a tree to protect the cars, but it was next to impossible to find refuge. When we got to our new Miami home, everything we brought in was a muddy mess. Right out of the gate, the horrendous weather seemed like a sign of things to come. There was definitely a storm front coming all right!

All we had to start things off in our new home were some mattresses on the floor, so I had to play set dresser again. I decided to furnish the house a little less expensively because in Miami you can get away with smoke and mirrors by using a lot of white—white drapes, white pillows, white sofas, and so on.

In a magazine, I saw a house in Bali that looked stunning. I wanted to re-create a similar look in our new house with teak furniture, white fabric, palm trees, fountains, candles—all very peaceful. I thought it would look oh-so Miami for the show. I researched and found a place locally that sold furniture. I got a great deal, with all of the furniture costing us only $35,000. It was perfect for the Miami look, since we basically lived on set. Quick, cheap, and looks good on TV!

After it was delivered and Terry walked into the house, he flipped out. He hated the chunky teak furniture and wanted a modern sleek look for the house. "Get this shit out of here," he demanded. "Call the guy at the store and tell him to take it back right now. What are you thinking!"

Men don't usually care about furniture, especially Terry. Men care about sex, food, money, and sleeping. Plus, Terry never complained about all of the dark furniture I put in the Willadel house. When I furnished it on my own, he never asked me to return any of it. He loved showing his house off and knew that I knew what I was doing when it came to decorating. Looking back, I don't think this was about the furniture. I think it was about finding stupid things that were wrong about me so he could excuse his cheating ways. Or maybe it was to make me feel inadequate and keep me busy so I wouldn't notice what he was doing behind my back. The argument created distance, and that distance enabled him to do what he really wanted to do. If the house was in disarray, we both wouldn't be there.

Returning the furniture caused a huge ruckus, and it sat in our garage as we negotiated a return. Meanwhile, we were set to begin shooting season three of *Hogan Knows Best* in two weeks and I had a huge home to furnish. I wished he'd had more compassion. Needless to say, I spent the next fourteen days basically living in my car and the main Levitz furniture showroom. It ended up being a costly mistake because I think they saw me coming! I thought Mom could shed some quick decorating light on the subject, but it was too hard to try to have her help from Los Angeles at the last minute. I decided to use a local decorator. He had a studio in the design district with lots of furniture on the floor. I bought most of the stuff he had because it was contemporary and available immediately. I really didn't have time now to worry about the price.

Terry liked the square modern look, so I went with it. It wasn't my cup of tea at all, and I became dependent on the decorator to do the house. I guess it looked all right, but it ended up being so expensive. I had a deadline and never intended on having all of the added frustration! At that point, I was in over my head. Finally, the house was decorated to Terry's liking. I was over it. I didn't even care anymore. I had so much else on my plate.

Once the house was decorated, we started taping the new season. Honestly, I felt the show looked terrible that year because it was shot against an all-white background looking bland and boring. Willadel was so colorful and warm looking.

I really had a gorgeous plan for the house at first—waterfalls, palms, white flowing drapes—but trying to please Terry and do the ultramod thing? I just couldn't figure out how to make the house look full with low, modern Italian furniture! Viewers who had watched the first two seasons of *Hogan Knows Best* were used to seeing bright colors and green trees on the show. Now, the only comfortable room in the entire house to sit in was a family room off the kitchen. Primarily, the entire family sat on one couch and two chairs for the entire third season. Our goal was to have new surroundings, but we were more confined than ever.

The heat in Miami was getting to me, and it had nothing to do with the weather.

Sleeping with the Frenemy?

The pressure of the show, kids' schedules, animals, new help, workmen at the door, twenty-eight-person film crew, and the kids' new friends caused a lot of behind-the-scenes fighting and bickering within our family during season three. It was like we were all in a pressure cooker with the cameras constantly rolling, wardrobe needing to be changed, getting the house ready for filming each day, and so on. And my day didn't end when the cameras were shut off. No, I was only at the halfway point. We also had Brooke's music career to contend with, and it was in full swing.

After we filmed all day I would take Brooke to the studio in Miami to work all night on her upcoming album. I'd literally sleep on a leather couch in the recording studio until six thirty in the morning, waking up every hour or so to check on Brooke and be a cheerleader for her. Then we'd rush back home and I'd have to be on-camera with VH1 at nine thirty A.M. When I got home from the recording studio, I would feed all the dogs and clean up the kitchen while Terry either slept, went to the gym, or simply woke up and got himself ready. I took a lot of static for not looking so good the last year in Miami. The tabloids relentlessly made fun of my outfits that I wore on-camera. With absolutely no time to shop, I wasn't looking or feeling so hot.

Brooke had become good friends with Christiane, the secretary from the label. First, Christiane began assisting Brooke. I was so busy getting settled into our new house in Miami and shooting the reality show that I couldn't handle every detail like I used to. At the time, Christiane was in her early thirties and Brooke was only nineteen, so it was great to have an adult with her from the record label. She assisted with autographing pictures and making sure the hotel reservations were made and the car service was on time, among other details like walking Brooke up to her room and getting her food. I always kept my interactions with Christiane professional. Brooke and Christiane had become good friends, and I let them do their thing. I was glad that Brooke had a companion on the road who could understand her workload and help her out a bit.

Their friendship didn't end on the road. When Brooke was back in Miami, Christiane would often sleep over at the house in Brooke's room. Brooke lived over the garage and had her own entrance with a lock on her door. Christiane slept in a separate bed in a loft in Brooke's garage apartment. Since Brooke's front door was close to the street, I told her to lock it at all times because anyone could hop the wall and break into her room. In Miami, you had to be extra careful. Sometimes, when Christiane was sleeping over, in the morning I'd walk across the courtyard to her room and the door would be unlocked. "Brooke, I told you to always lock the door!" I hollered.

"I did, Mom," she answered. "I don't know what you're talking about."

Oh, that's typical of kids, I thought.

Weird things continued to happen that year in Miami—things that were hard to pinpoint, and I questioned my own sanity!

There was a round table and chairs in our master bedroom in Miami, and I was sitting there one afternoon trying to plan Brooke's tour. I had two big bookcases that were ten feet tall. On the very top shelf, I had placed beautifully framed photos of me and the children. The other shelf had a collection of beautiful glass vases. I noticed something that didn't look right. I stood on a chair and was surprised to see all of the framed photos of the kids and me turned over facedown. Did they fall over? There are no earthquakes in Florida. The vases and everything else were where I left them. Why were only the photos lying facedown? Did the maid knock them over? It was too high up for the maid to dust. And with seventeen thousand square feet of house to clean, it's probably the last place she was worried about. It just didn't add up.

From that time on, I started watching Terry more closely. Every morning as soon as he got up, he would attach his fanny pack to his waist, stuffed with his wallet and two cell phones. Even if Terry got up at six A.M. to make coffee, he would put the fanny pack on just to go downstairs. One day, when he came up a few minutes later holding his coffee cup, I asked him, "Why do you always have to take that fanny pack with you every time you go downstairs?"

"I might have to make a phone call," he said.

"At six in the morning?" I shot back. "Why do you need two cell phones anyway?"

"I don't get good reception on one of them."

Terry always seemed to have an answer for everything. Many times at night he would pull into the driveway and he'd sit in his Mercedes for a while, talking on his cell phone. Once or twice I understand that you're in the middle of a call and you don't want to hang up and come right in. After a while, though, it was beginning to become a habit and it raised a red flag. One night I saw his headlights on for fifteen to twenty minutes and ran outside and told him to come in. Instead, he stayed out there for another twenty minutes. When Terry finally came inside, I asked him, a bit pissed off, "Why didn't you just take the call in here?"

"I was already on the call and was comfortable inside the car." Excuses, excuses!

Terry kept putting distance between us as well as with the people working alongside him on the show. During the day, he wouldn't eat catered lunch with the crew. Instead, he'd always go out to eat by "himself" at a local Mexican restaurant, or so I thought. In actuality he was probably dining on Christiane's lap!

When I was with Brooke in New York recording her

music, I expressed my concern about the release date of her album, which was something that I didn't agree with. When I got back to Miami, Terry confronted me about it. The *only* person who heard my conversation was Christiane. I asked Terry the golden question, "How do you even know about this?" I caught him off guard and after some stuttering he explained that Christiane told her boss, and then he told Terry. This was the tip of the iceberg. *Too weird!*

As Nick's schedule grew more crowded, with his getting his GED and a sponsorship with Dodge, I was busier than ever. So Terry began accompanying Brooke to the recording studio. I was thankful because the hours were so bad. What I didn't realize was that as he went more and more to the studios, he became closer friends with Brooke's producers. When I went with Brooke, I'd make her tea with honey and listen in to the session, or sleep just outside her vocal booth on a black leather sofa until she needed me again. But when Terry went with Brooke, they put Brooke in a recording booth and then they'd all hang out in a separate room away from her, partying with a steady stream of women. I never knew any of this until we were close to wrapping the last season of *Hogan Knows Best*. Let's just say, the walls had eyes. Brooke worked so hard on her debut album, *Undiscovered*. When it was released in October 2006, it seemed a shame that the label owner didn't have a solid marketing plan behind it. It was clear that they were more or less just counting on it selling on the heels of our fame and television show. Well, the album fell flat on its face because it had no promotion. I asked Terry to help us to get the label to promote Brooke's album properly. He pretty much soft-pedaled the situation. I think he didn't want to put a rift in his relationship with the head of the label because he had a few other big deals riding with them for himself and he didn't want to rock the boat. Watching the album fail and the record label and her dad do nothing about it was devastating to Brooke. I would come to find out that there was even more to the story behind the scenes.

For New Year's Eve 2007, our family made plans to go to the Forge, a fancy and trendy restaurant in Miami. Brooke felt sorry for Christiane because she had no plans for New Year's and insisted that she come out with us. Brooke let her borrow a dress, and we called the restaurant and made room for one more at our table. While at the Forge, the wine was flowing, with bottles of red and white on our table at all times. I sat on one side of Terry while Christiane sat on the other. I noticed that the more the wine flowed, the cozier Christiane and Terry became with each other. Throughout dinner Terry kept reaching over and refilling Christiane's glass with red wine and then he'd fill his own, never once pouring me any white. After dinner, Brooke and Nick went to meet some of their friends at another place down the street, while Terry, Christiane, and I went to the disco that was attached the restaurant. At the club, while we waited for our drinks Christiane excused herself and went to the restroom, and a couple seconds later Terry excused himself to go to the men's room. The drinks came, and I sat alone at the table waiting for Terry and Christiane. Ten minutes went by, fifteen, twenty— they were gone for so long. My cell phone rang and Brooke told me that she and Nick needed to be picked up at another club right away. I couldn't find Terry or Christiane anywhere. I paid the check and left the drinks on the table! I went to the ladies' room—no Christiane. I went back to the restaurant area and they weren't there, either. I went outside the club to the valet to get the car. A few moments later Terry came outside and Christiane resurfaced shortly after that. *This is really odd,* I thought. *Where were they for almost a half hour?*

With Terry's behavior on New Year's Eve along with all that was happening in our private life I couldn't help but begin to think that Terry was having an affair. Again? All the signs were staring me directly in the face. *Is it Christiane?* I wondered. *Was it her makeup on the pillow? Was the reason Brooke's door wasn't locked at night because Christiane was sneaking out to see Terry? Was the reason Christiane didn't have plans on New Year's Eve because her boyfriend had a family—us?*

I had my suspicions, but no proof. That night when we got home from the Forge, I asked Brooke if she thought Terry was having an affair with Christiane. "No, I totally trust her," Brooke said, reassuring me. "She's my best friend. There's no way."

I thought Christiane liked me. Obviously she liked my husband more! Christiane was a good shoulder for him to cry on. She was also younger and fresher than I was. And if our marriage was going to fail, she assumed that she would be the next in line, I guess. Looking at the resources we had, Christiane knew she could possibly hit the jackpot!

Sign Language

When a man is good-looking, rich, powerful, famous, and . . . thinks the grass is greener on the other side, this is a recipe for disaster in any marriage. A man who is more in demand, especially one who says he's not happy at home, is more likely to cheat. Women throw themselves at men who are in the public eye, and it's almost too easy for them to stray. Also, highly successful men are used to taking risks. They get an adrenaline rush from the excitement when they are risking it all, including their marriage. This rush becomes addictive. They view love as a game and want to keep it exciting at all times, and it's happening a lot now. Single women pursuing these men, luring them, thinking nothing of the kids or the outcome for them. The temptation for men is too hard to resist, especially when a woman makes it her mission in life to be with a married man.

I know this type of man. I was married to one for almost twenty-four years.

If your husband is always distracted, distant, and mentally not present or aware, you might want to look at him more closely. I use "present" and "aware" because those are words that Terry *now* has tattooed on his wrists. I believe he realized that he should have been more present and aware during our marriage. During the end of our marriage, he always made me feel like I was the one who was falling apart. He said that I cussed too much, I drank too much, I was too fat, didn't work out enough, and so on. I think he would strategically pick me apart, so I would have low self-esteem. It was a typical attempt to throw me off guard. I even noticed that he seemed bored with our family. He didn't want to plan any vacations or anything in the future. "Where do you see yourself in five years?" I asked him.

"I don't know," he said. "I can't even answer that. I'm taking it one day at a time."

If you think your husband is cheating, there are signs—a different type of sign language. Take the following signs at face value because they're pretty much classic telltale symptoms of cheating. And don't be afraid. Open your eyes to them because you deserve to know the truth.

- Your husband has a sudden increase in time spent away from home.
- He has decreased sexual interest in you.
- He leaves the house or goes to another room to talk on his cell phone, blaming it on background noise, lack of reception, and so on.
- He sits inside of his car upon arrival at the home and talks on his phone for five more minutes. He knows he can't finish that call inside in front of his family.
- He asks about your schedule more often than usual. He wants to know where you are going, but then is noncommittal when you try to pin him down to a schedule.
- He has more cash on him than normal without any accountability.
- He tries not to get to close to you because he smells like another woman's perfume.
- When he answers the phone in front of you, he gets a lot of "wrong numbers."
- He makes frequent trips to the store and has lots of late business meetings.
- His friends cover for him and his whereabouts.
- He sleeps in a separate bedroom or on the sofa.
- He doesn't make any eye contact when talking with you.

- He has constant mood swings and is always short with you.
- He makes you feel like *you're* the one who is falling apart.

If you think your husband is cheating, don't make accusations. This will only make him take being sneaky to the next level. He will hide the affair to throw you off the scented trail. Seek the advice of a private investigator. As I talk about things like a private investigator, it hits me as being surreal. I never dreamed that I would have to have my husband followed.

Some women turn a blind eye or they actually cheat on their husbands to get back at them. I wasn't capable of having a sexual relationship with another man while I was married. I didn't have time to have girlfriends, let alone a guy I could be sneaking away with. First of all, it was wrong; and even if it had been convenient or the opportunity had presented itself, I still wouldn't have acted on it. No matter how bad my marriage got, I'm not of that fiber. It takes strength of character and an ability to honor a commitment! My opinion of women who cheat with married men is that they are selfish and careless, and they are homewreckers. My first priority was keeping my family together and keeping my children happy.

If you are ever considering cheating on a spouse, stop and think about the consequences. It's a gamble. Think about everything you've worked for—your home, cars, savings accounts, everything monetary—and then think about everyone who loves and respects you—your children, parents, friends, the people you love—and be willing to put it *all* down on a gaming table where you can lose it all in just one move. *Why would you risk everything?* Who out there besides your family is worth that kind of risk? Is a ten-second orgasm really worth it? It is selfish and destructive to everyone involved, and if you're the one who is guilty, you're going to have to live with that choice forever. You're going to have to look in the mirror at the guilty face staring back and figure out how to live with your lie. I could never take a risk like that. But in the end I had to deal with the results of someone else doing that to me. It was painful and life-changing.

Chapter 10

THE LIAR'S DEN

ROM January through June 2007 we shot
season three of *Hogan Knows Best*. It was the
final season of our show, but we didn't know it when we began
production at the beginning of that year. While most shows get
canceled by the network due to low ratings, we had a different
ending. The ratings were there. The family unity was gone.

It was clear to me that Terry was living a double life. I just
didn't know with whom or how to know for sure. I was terrified
of getting caught if I followed him or snooped through his stuff.
So, I relied on the age old line "Time will tell!"

One of the episodes that we did toward the end of the season
was a scene between Terry and me at a marriage counselor's

office. Here is a diary entry that gives some insight into how I was feeling before going to marriage counseling:

> *It's been as stressful as I can ever remember! I am trying to hold it together, but I am so close to giving up on everything. We have no fun, no lifestyle or even a calm friendly conversation. We're just going through the motions. We don't even talk; it's bitching, whining, complaining, tiredness, soreness, or arguing. I can't wait to finish filming Season 3 and get through this last season, just to get away! I'm sick of all the BS. I want to move out of this monster Miami house, regain my composure, and move to Cali! Try to regain a life together again!*

Terry and I had never been to a marriage counselor before even though friends and family members had suggested it to us over the years. I had even brought up the idea to Terry again. But he didn't see how it could help our situation. He couldn't wrap his head around the thought of somebody who was so removed from the entertainment business and wrestling giving us advice on how to fix our life. He felt strongly that if they didn't understand that integral part of our lives, then they could never understand us or our problems. He also didn't trust them not to run to the tabloids with our personal and private details. I just felt trapped. While we were shooting in Miami our relationship was always up and down. There was never any continuity. Terry and I would get along. Then we would fight. We would get along. Then we would fight. I thought it was because we had so much stuff going on in our life with cameras, kids, and stress. Not getting along seemed par for the course. I didn't analyze it any deeper than that. He'd be sad, then happy. I never knew if it was genuine or not.

The producers of our reality show felt that all married couples who have been together this long fight, come back together, and then fight again. They felt it was common in most marriages, so maybe we should go to marriage counseling on the show.

Through the course of that week when we were shooting in the marriage counselor's office, they basically wanted to peel back the skin of our relationship and ask some pretty personal questions. If we had been in a counseling session with no cameras rolling, I would have welcomed answering the tough questions. I wouldn't have held back at all because who knows? It might have made things better between us. However, this was being done for national TV, and I wasn't ready to rip the lid off our personal problems.

At the end of the week, Terry started getting serious with the sessions. He was shooting darts, but I wasn't firing back. I was acting as though this was going in one ear and out the other, but underneath it all it was making me feel very uncomfortable. When the cameras were off, Terry and I began to fight about what was discussed in the therapy sessions. While I thought that going to a marriage counselor might actually help, he took what was discussed to heart and copped an attitude about it. It derailed us and didn't help us get any closer. I was mad that he would try to embarrass me in front of the crew, in front of the world!

• • •

We ended up going to three weeks of marriage counseling sessions. One of the exercises during the sessions was for us to write a poem to each other about how we felt. Looking back, and knowing what was really going on that whole year, how could Terry have meant the words of his poem in a genuine way? He didn't. It was only something that made him look good on television. However, when Terry read the poem out loud to me, I was brought to tears. I thought that maybe we really had a tender moment. Maybe I had been misjudging him. It gave me a strand of hope. As always, he made me doubt my own feelings, my behavior, my attitude, and second-guess my thoughts and actions. That's what control freaks do. They brainwash you. Here's what he had written:

> *The first time I saw you, I saw your feet* [I wear a
>   size 11] *and then I saw you.*
> *Let's have our first drink and then you might think,*
>   *I am the one for you.*
> *You lied about your car, you didn't know I was a*
>   *star.*
> *So you left the bar and I had no idea you would go*
>   *so far.*
> *In the end we would turn out to be more than just*
>   *friends.*
> *So I did a knee bend, so we could stay together till*
>   *the end.*
> *I love you too, so whatcha gonna do?*

After he read that poem, I began to think that maybe therapy *could* bring us together, be the jump start that we needed. Well, it turned out to be wishful thinking. Shortly after that episode, Terry went back to his old ways. This time, it was just blatant and more disrespectful than before. He was sleeping in another room every night. I begged him to sleep in our bed, but he told me that he liked the other bed better. He didn't like the dogs being in bed with us. I even locked them in the laundry room, trying to make him happy. But he still didn't sleep with me. So many excuses! And the baffling behavior didn't end there. He made little or no eye contact with me. We barely had civilized conversations. When we would get ready in the morning to shoot the show, he would stare straight into the mirror and not even look at me. He even started using a separate bathroom, further separating us.

Back then, if we had any sexual relations, it was mainly oral sex from me to him. He would lie there on his back lifeless and I'd do all the work. Most of the time he didn't even want sex, probably because he was getting sex elsewhere and he was wiped out by the time he came home to me. But when he wanted sex, he wanted to try new things with me that I had never done with him before. *Where did he learn that new trick?* I wondered. He'd turn the TV on at bedtime and go directly to a premium channel—porn! He went to it like radar!

It certainly wasn't the first time we had watched porn together. He had put porn on every now and then in a hotel room. But this became a regular nightly thing. If I was tired and I wasn't in the mood, Terry would get pissed off. He became angry if I wasn't interested. And if it didn't go his way, he would curse at me, stomp his feet, and go sleep in the other bedroom. The next morning, he would treat me badly if we didn't have sex the night before. *Is this all that our marriage has come to after so many years?* I thought. *What a heartless relationship this is becoming.* Sure, sex is important in a marriage, but when we shut the last light off after a long day and got into bed, it would have been nice to have a little chitchat or at least go to bed *together.*

Terry's fanny pack was back around his waist at all times. In fact, the producers did an episode on *Hogan Knows Best* where they wanted to know what was inside Terry's infamous fanny pack. Of course, he cleaned it out before they filmed it. Inside he only had toothpicks, business cards, and his wallet. How cute. Normally, he had two or three cell phones, pills out the ass, and a lot of cash!

Toward that last part of filming we would go out to dinner or on the boat and Christiane was always with us. I thought she was there because she was Brooke's friend, but it was really just convenient for Terry to hook up with her. I remember how he always manipulated me into thinking *I* was a crappy person! I drank too much, I cursed too much, I always left and drove to the other house or got on a plane and flew away. Honestly, I left because I was scared. We were in such abusive verbal fights. Sure, I would say, "Fuck off," but I would never directly call him a dirty name. He called me a "dumb cunt!" This let me know that at this point he had no respect for me or our marriage.

I think Terry had Christiane at his beck and call and it was to his benefit to pick a fight with me. He knew what buttons to push and how to piss me off. He also knew that I was the one who would always walk away and often leave for the weekend after an argument. If it was Friday and we were done filming, instead of spending a nice weekend together, he would pick a juicy fight with me. I wanted to be left alone and preferred spending the weekend with my animals as company, so I'd get in my car and go back to our old house. He knew that if he did certain things, I would leave and it would give him a free weekend. How he lived with his conscience, I will never know.

Things were also taking a turn for the worse with Brooke's music career and her relationship with her record label. It was clear that Terry wasn't sticking up for Brooke, and he was more focused on his own deals with the label owner. An energy drink, online gaming, frozen food line, boxing promotions, a toy robot, a TV show, and more. Terry refused to speak to the label head about any glitches, because he didn't want anything to upset that business rapport or any of his own deals. Terry was being such a jerk. I was puzzled by the changes that were going on with him.

The label continued to treat Brooke poorly, and it became evident that they weren't putting any marketing or promotion behind her upcoming album. I didn't have a platform to speak, and Terry had monopolized the label owner and taken over that business relationship for his own gain. Brooke was trying to handle a lot of the business on her own, but her father was undermining her by putting his own deals first. At that point, I think Terry thought Brooke was just a fly in the ointment.

As soon as Brooke and I confronted the label owner, and ruffled his feathers, Terry got angry with us. Now, it wasn't just Terry and me at odds at home, but he and Brooke were arguing as well. Brooke came home one night, irate about the way the label was handling her business. She told Terry how upset she was and about all the horrible things being said behind the scenes. She even told the label that she was going to quit.

• • •

THE VERY NEXT NIGHT BROOKE WAS AT THE FORGE RESTAURANT eating and in walked Terry, the label owner, and Eric Bischoff. They were laughing and sat down to have drinks. She was amazed that her own father could be laughing and having drinks with her boss, when just the night before she broke down and told him about how hurt she was by what his label *wasn't* doing to help her. Terry clearly wasn't the least bit concerned that Brooke was at odds with this man. This behavior and his lack of loyalty to Brooke painted him in a different light to me, different than I had ever seen him before.

That night, Brooke came home and wrote "liar" on the front door of our home. She didn't want to speak to her dad and wanted to quit the record label. Brooke was in a frenzy, upset like I had never seen her upset before. I couldn't believe that Terry could do this to his own daughter. He was acting blind to it all. He couldn't have cared less if she was upset, because *his* business deals came first now.

Brooke wanted to immediately jump on a plane and head to Los Angeles. She begged me to come with her. When I realized there was no calming her down, I went with her to the West Coast. During the plane ride to L.A., Brooke and I both wrote in our journals. I didn't even tell Terry I left with her, but with all the events that led up to this point, I certainly had a lot on my mind to write about. We were both mad at Terry. We both felt betrayed. We both felt disappointed. We both had so many things to say. How could somebody act this way to his own family? I wrote all the things that came to my mind. My pen just flowed. I wrote down a list of words describing the kind of person I felt Terry had become.

- *Abusive*
- *Controlling*
- *Selfish*
- *Demeaning*
- *Disrespectful*
- *Not trustworthy*
- *Unfaithful*
- *Liar*
- *Childish*
- *Noncommunicative*
- *User*
- *Dependent*
- *Depressive*
- *Manipulative*
- *Plotting*
- *Secretive*
- *Self-centered*
- *Conceited*
- *Gloating*
- *Calculating*
- *Insecure*
- *Sex addict*
- *Violent*
- *Sneaky*
- *Unhappy*
- *Cheater*
- *Back stabber*

- *Rude*
- *Delusional*
- *Victimizer*
- *Self-consumed*
- *Insensitive*
- *On edge*
- *Negative*
- *Fear of change*
- *Possessive*
- *Brainwasher*
- *Antagonistic*
- *No morals*
- *No sense of family*

I reread the list while I was writing this book, I still feel that Terry seems to represent every single one of these characteristics. The words just filled my head. I couldn't write fast enough! It was scary. When you go through the list, it's clear that these are the signs of a pathological liar and a narcissist.

I had been victimized for two decades by a narcissist.

AS THE SHOW ENDED, I WAS IN SUCH TURMOIL WITH TERRY. THE arguing got so bad we could hardly keep a civil game face on for the cameras. When I landed in Los Angeles, I didn't want to go back. I told him to forget about the show. I was done.

Terry called me and said that if I didn't come back and do the reshoots that VH1 was threatening to sue: I just wanted to die. Honestly, I'd rather have drank bleach than gone back to face him again. I couldn't pretend to be in a good mood and do an episode with him that was supposed to be happy when I really wanted to poke his eyes out! I decided not to do it. I realized it was another dangling of the carrot to get me to come back to Florida. But as he persisted about the possible lawsuit, I got scared. Very reluctantly I went back to Florida to finish the season.

In order to stay positive, I needed to stay numb emotionally—like nothing bothered me. Because when I thought about everything in my life that I was missing, it made me so sad. I missed the emotional support of my husband. The love. The friendship. I didn't have any of that. It was gone. Everything in our life was falling apart, and I kept making excuses. I tried to figure out the problem. Why was Terry acting so cold and removed? Why was everything so difficult? I had always looked forward to the day when the kids were all grown up and Terry and I could get through the empty-nest stage together. I wasn't sure if that would ever be. There seemed to be so many holes in our relationship, and so much suspicion on my end regarding his infidelity, and it was getting more and more difficult to keep it together. But I had no proof of anything, and I felt stuck; it wasn't in me to leave yet, and I was paralyzed with fear and confusion. So I just went through the motions, doing whatever I had to do to stay positive, but I was so tired and drained.

After we completed the reshoots, I eventually spoke to one of the executives at VH1, to explain I just couldn't do season four of *Hogan Knows Best*. I also asked if I hadn't come back if they were, in fact, going to approach me legally. The executive had never intended anything like that. Terry had just lied to me to get me to come back to Florida, to control me. They expected me to finish the season. That was all.

Over the course of that year Terry wasn't wrestling as much and spending a lot more time working on the show. Terry said that a lot of deals were going to come through, but nothing seemed to be clicking. I just kept seeing money going out and not coming in. If we didn't cut back then, I foresaw problems down the road. We needed to make a change before the bottom fell out. It was too expensive to keep the house in Miami, so we put it up for sale.

When we sold the Miami house, I knew the kids and I were going right to L.A. The kids and I didn't want to go back to Willadel. Even though we had a big beautiful house in Clearwater, we were burned out. Clearwater had nothing to offer, as far as the entertainment business. We needed to be in California, in L.A., the entertainment machine.

I wanted more than ever to have a place back in L.A. I dreamed of being closer to my family again, and the kids really wanted to move, too. I always felt it would have helped Terry's floundering career. Sylvester Stallone and Arnold Schwarzenegger lived there and they were his friends. I also believed it would have helped Brooke's music career and Nick's career in movies. It only made sense for all of us to get a small place on the West Coast now.

Terry knew I didn't want to settle back in Clearwater, so he finally agreed to let us move. However, every single time I found something suitable in L.A., Terry told me that he wouldn't rent without seeing it. But then he never made himself available to look. How convenient! Control, control, control! This move was like pulling teeth. I finally decided to rent a furnished house and put our belongings in storage when the time came.

I started packing up the house in Miami. I had fifteen moving guys and my regular housekeeper, and I hired four housekeepers from an agency. I had never met them before and had second thoughts about even letting them in my house, but I was behind schedule and forged ahead with them anyway.

The kids and Terry never helped me during the move. As usual, the kids never had to do chores—clean their rooms or take out the trash. Terry always excused them from that and made me seem like I was asking for the moon. It was just easier to let them go, and not start a fight with Terry. A lot of the burden of running the home fell on me. That morning, Terry woke up and, as usual, went to the gym for three hours and then was off to lunch at the Mexican restaurant he loved. Brooke was busy working at the music studio. Nick and his friend Danny Jacobs were playing in the pool. I spearheaded the entire move on an extremely hot August Miami afternoon with a moving crew of twenty that barely spoke English. Navigating all seventeen thousand square feet alone with strangers!

When the time came for me to pack up Terry's closet, he didn't want me to pack any of his stuff.

"What are you doing?" he asked. "Don't pack any of these clothes. Hang them back up."

"Why? We're moving," I shot back.

"I'm going to pack my own stuff and send it on another truck," he said.

I was confused because there was no valid excuse for why he didn't want me to pack his belongings. "Terry, escrow closes in two more days, and we need to get this stuff out of here. The truck is leaving in two hours."

"Don't worry about it. I don't want anybody touching my shit."

He ended up letting me pack some of his long-sleeved sweaters and jackets for L.A. He basically pacified me with that. Later that night, I wanted to get my jewelry out of the safe. We had two tiny cubicle safes that basically someone could walk away with, especially a strong moving guy. When I asked Terry to open the safe, he paused for a minute.

"My jewelry's in there, right?" I asked.

"Yeah," he responded. "Give me a minute." He acted as though he didn't remember which safe my belongings were in.

"It's in this one," I said, pointing to the silver one and not the black one. "It's always been in the silver one with the stickers on the front."

I had forgotten the code to the safe. I only kept my jewelry in there, and when I wanted it, Terry would open it up for me. After he opened the safe, I reached in to grab my things and along with my stuff I pulled out a crinkly white CVS bag that was quite heavy. I opened it and all I saw were stacks of $100 bills. "Did you rob a bank?" I asked, shocked. "Where did you get all this money from?"

The most we ever had in the safe at one time was $5,000 cash. It turned out that there was $50,000 in the CVS bag. Terry explained that he took half of his recent salary for an autograph signing in cash because there wasn't a good turnout at the event and he decided to let the promoter off the hook for the other half. I knew that it was a lie because Terry had a contract for

$100,000 and he was *all* business when it came to money. There was no way he would opt to take half after traveling and doing the signing. I asked why he didn't tell me about it, and he didn't have a concrete answer. Not to mention the fact that he seemed very nervous I'd found it.

Once the trucks drove out, I spent the rest of that evening cleaning up, leaving fresh flowers I'd ordered and bottles of wine on the counter for the man who purchased our house. He was a Hollywood producer/director and I wanted to make sure the house looked like a model home. He bought some of the furniture, too, so I went through each room putting the finishing touches on each of the pieces. He was going to do a walk-through before the final signatures to close the deal the next day.

That evening when everything was done, I was absolutely exhausted, hot, sweaty, and dirty. I just wanted to take a shower, pack my travel bag, and go to bed! Instead of Terry hugging me or thanking me for all of my hard work and preparation, he picked a fight with me about which porch lights I had left on! I wanted to leave most of them on so the house looked pretty that night, in case the new owner drove by. Looking back, he probably didn't want them all on so he could sneak out with Christiane. It was the final fucking straw! I said, "Whatever, fuck it!," and went to bed crying and alone.

The next morning, I didn't stay for the walk-through. I left before Terry woke up and hung out in the lobby of a hotel until the walk-through was completed, being responsible enough to wait in case they had questions or I needed to sign something. I waited four hours in the hot lobby. Once I left, I didn't want one reason to have to return! I got the final okay from the broker that the papers were signed. The house closed and the buyer was very happy. I called myself a taxi and went to the Miami airport. I had to hurry to L.A. to find a warehouse to store the belongings from our Miami house because the trucks would be there in five days.

In July 2007, I FINALLY SETTLED INTO THE HOME WE RENTED IN Westwood, California, near Beverly Hills. It was a cute Spanish-style home that wasn't big, but a perfect transition home for our family. I asked Terry, who was staying at our Willadel home, when he was going to join us in Los Angeles. He told me that he was going to stay in Clearwater for his birthday and then fly out afterward. *He's not coming for another week?* I thought. *He's spending his birthday without us? What an ass!* Even with Terry being so rude and mean, I still reached out to him for his birthday. When I called him, it sounded like he was partying it up! Laughing and with friends over, he didn't miss me at all.

I was in L.A. getting ready to put Brooke out on a tour and was exhausted from the move and traveling. I called Terry and asked if he and Nick would be coming to L.A. for my birthday on August 24, only a week away. He told me that they had decided to stay in Florida for a "boys' week." Nick also planned to hit a few towns with his friends John Graziano and Danny Jacobs for some drifting events (drifting is a precision driving technique). He was on the East Coast first, so he returned to Tampa a few days before Terry's birthday and then left right after for the West Coast. The boys spent a few days with me in California, but couldn't stay for my birthday, as a drift event was going on in Tampa and they had to get back.

I did think it was odd that Terry didn't let me put his clothes on the truck. I just couldn't imagine that he wasn't going to come out with his family to California. I believed him when he said that he had stuff to do in Tampa but would be right behind us. I had no time to question it because Brooke was touring with her music and Nick was touring with his racing.

Meanwhile, back at the ranch, I received a phone call from one of Nick's old girlfriends. "Linda, is Brooke in Clearwater?" she asked.

"No, she's actually in Seattle performing this weekend. Why?"

"Are you sure?"

"Yes, I am sure," I responded. "My brother, Joey, went there with her."

"Well, I'm sitting here at Shephard's on the beach and I just saw your husband go by on a Jet Ski with a blonde on the back that looked just like Brooke."

"Well, it's not Brooke. Brooke is in Seattle!"

"Then who was it?"

"That's exactly my question."

All I can tell you is that it was *not* Christiane; she was a brunette. Terry was probably done with Christiane and already on to his new girlfriend, Jennifer McDaniel. The sickening thing was that he was still married to me, and I was still trying to keep our marriage together. That was why he didn't want to come to Los Angeles to spend my birthday with me; or why he didn't want me to come back to Florida and interrupt his "boys' week." Terry probably told her he was already separated.

I spent my forty-eighth birthday completely alone. I did get a knock on the door from a flower delivery guy. He had two bunches of roses in his hands in tired, cheap little vases. The roses looked all raggedy with thorns, like he bought them from someone at a freeway off-ramp. One bunch was yellow and one was red—Hulkamania. There were also two cards that both read the same exact thing: "Happy Birthday. Love, Terry." "Happy Birthday. Love, Terry." *Wow, that was creative*, I thought. Terry usually sent me beautiful roses and flower bouquets for events. This time, he missed the mark sadly. His heart was *not* into it. I was just so pissed at him for not coming out for my birthday. And for him to think that two last-minute crappy arrangements would make up for it obviously proved that he didn't even care!

The next morning I went to get my hair done. The stylist proceeded to dye my hair a horrible khaki green color, when attempting to add lowlights. I was so upset. Crappy flowers, no Terry or Nick, Brooke gone performing, and now green hair! Plus, I was so depressed—alone in a new house. Why was everything so hard? What happened to my family? Why am I alone on everything? I sat at the kitchen table trying to learn how to use my new computer. The phone rang at four thirty in the afternoon. It was Terry calling. *Why is he calling me?* I wondered. He had been picking fights on the phone with me all week long, being cocky and arrogant. I wasn't going to answer, but I decided to because I thought maybe he was going to finally join me. I always tried to see the glass half full. I answered with an optimistic and happy, "Hello?"

"Linda, Nick has been in an accident."

"What? Oh my God! Oh my God! Is he okay?"

"It's really bad. He hit a tree."

"Is he alive? Is he alive?"

"I don't know. I don't know."

I dropped the phone and fell to my knees. I don't know if

I experienced temporary insanity or fainted and came to or what, but I was absolutely overwhelmed by the anxiety. I couldn't talk. I couldn't breathe in or breathe out. I had never experienced this kind of fear in my life. My knees and legs were like jelly. I tried to call my mom for help, but of course I dialed the wrong number and couldn't get through. I couldn't see . . . couldn't think. I was alone. Then Terry called back. "The ambulance is here," he said. "They're cutting Nick out of the car."

"Oh my God," I screamed to the Lord. "Please let Nick be alive!!"

"Who else was with him?" I asked, frantically.

"John was in the car."

"Is John alive?" I asked. I couldn't believe I was saying "alive."

"I don't know. The paramedics are taking him away in the helicopter." I was in shock.

I was three thousand miles away in California. I needed to fly back home to see Nick and John immediately. Nick has a rare blood type—the same one I have—so if anything happened, I knew he would need my blood. I still didn't know if my son or his friend were alive. I begged God to please not take my Nick!

I wasn't thinking straight and drove to nearby Santa Monica airport and begged them for a private jet. They claimed they had one, but when ten P.M. came, they still didn't know if they had a chartered jet available for sure. My phone was dying, and I was alone with my sixteen-year-old dog, Foxy. I still didn't know Nick's fate or John's. I was sick about what I would find out when I got home to Florida. I called my wealthy neighbors in Miami and asked if they could find me a plane. They found me a private jet that I so desperately needed. I was on a seventeen-passenger jet with just me and my dog, and it was the longest flight and night of my life. At that point, I couldn't care less how much it cost!

The Straw That Broke the Camel's Back

When I landed in Florida, the limo driver had word that they had released Nick from the hospital and that he was home. Thank you, God! I walked up the back stairs of our Willadel home and into Nick's bedroom. He had cuts and bruises and was wearing a sling. His eyes looked like they were in shock, and they watered when he saw me. Terry was in the room along with a lawyer!

"Linda, I know you must be anxious to know what happened," the attorney said, "but you can't speak to Nick about the accident."

I had no idea what the hell was going on. I didn't know the facts behind the accident. I didn't know why there was a lawyer in our house at seven A.M. I remember looking around at the bedroom and noticing that it looked like Nick had been entertaining his friends for a month straight. Empty Coke cans, potato chip wrappers, McDonald's wrappers, wet bathing suits and towels all over the floor—it was a mess!

If Terry had been there all week long, did he even wander up the steps to check on the boys? I thought. Obviously, his attention was on something else, possibly with big boobs. It really pissed me off because I knew Terry wasn't supervising them and that was probably the reason they got into the accident in the first place. Also, I never knew of Nick driving the yellow sports car before, and I later learned he had been driving the car the entire day before with Terry's permission. Not to mention that Nick had a restricted driver's license at the time of the accident. He had received three speeding tickets. And one of those tickets— the one where Nick was driving the fastest—he had gotten with his father in the passenger seat. Terry claims he was sleeping! I don't know anyone who could sleep while going over 100 miles per hour in a car with a sixteen-year-old driving. Do you? I'd be freaking out! One of the stipulations on the restricted license was that Nick was not allowed to drive after dark.

"Terry, the accident happened at seven thirty P.M. your time and it gets dark at eight," I said. "Why was Nick even on the road just leaving for the restaurant at that time? When they left the restaurant, he would have been driving on a restricted license after dark with *your* permission, Terry. Explain that to me!"

He couldn't. He told me that he was advised by the lawyer not to speak about anything. I was his mother, for God's sake. Well, that made things pretty convenient for Terry, not to have to explain anything to me.

There were many questions swirling around in my mind. But I did find out from one of the boys that they thought they had seen a blonde at the house earlier that week, and that might have been the same blonde on the Jet Ski a few days earlier.

We had to turn our focus to John and his well-being, so that afternoon our whole family went to the hospital to see how he was doing. He was in bad shape—much worse shape than we had anticipated. During the accident, he wasn't wearing a seat belt and had popped up out of the front seat and hit his head, suffering a brain injury. He remained unconscious and we feared for his life. We didn't know if we were going to lose him or not. It was surreal; we just couldn't believe this was really happening.

I had just seen John with Nick a week before in California

having fun in my pool at my house. I couldn't believe he was now lying in a hospital fighting for his life. I tried to console his mom, sister, and the rest of his family.

Terry told me that we would probably end up having a humongous lawsuit over this and explained that I should meet with a lawyer he had hired to go over some things. With all of the negative events leading up to the accident, I really didn't have any respect left for Terry. I was just going along with whatever I had to for Nick's sake. I was meeting with these lawyers because I was worried about my son and his fate. I couldn't believe Terry seemed primarily worried about being sued at a time like this! I hated Terry so much. I knew we had to have lawyers because it was an auto accident and Nick was driving. But I was worried about his fate, his life—not the damn lawsuit. They can have everything we owned; I just didn't want to lose John to death, or my son to jail.

Also at this time, I met with a lawyer Terry hired for the whole family. This lawyer kept insisting that the documents were part of a financial planning strategy. *Financial planning?* I thought.

Two months went by and Terry asked me if I ever looked over the documents. I told him I didn't understand why I needed my own attorney. If this was financial planning for us, why couldn't we use the same lawyer? None of this made any sense to me. He told me that it was an estate plan and that signing this document would help protect our assets. It just seemed weird that none of our original financial people were involved, but a new lawyer was handling it.

August, September, and October 2007 were spent in pure grief over John at the hospital. Our family dropped everything in our lives to be there every day, all living together at Willadel.

We tried to help John's mother and her kids. I was overwhelmed worrying about John's fate and Nick's fate. I finally called a lawyer. After I read the paperwork, he said that this was basically a marital agreement and it had nothing to do with financial planning. The documents Terry had given me were a completely different thing. Once I signed these papers we would stay married, but divvy up the monies as though we were divorced. I hung up the phone and just sat there thinking, appalled that Terry could lie to me so badly.

I was shocked. The fact that he was this calculating—to present me with papers like these—at a time like this—was unconscionable. Clearly, Terry was more concerned about how he could survive this with the least damage. This gave him an excuse to take it a step further. I realized that I needed to start looking for a divorce lawyer. Through Terry's actions and behavior, he gave me the answer I had needed, the final piece of the puzzle that confirmed just what kind of person he really was and that was it! He had been planning to leave me all along.

Chapter Eleven

END OF AN ERA

ERRY LANDED A JOB WITH NBC ON THE SHOW *American Gladiators,* which was shot in Los Angeles—the one place I thought he didn't want to be. I think Terry thought this would take him to a higher level financially and that's one of the reasons he wanted me to sign a midnuptial agreement. He was already preparing to split assets and discontinue sharing any future income. Huh! What a kick in the teeth! I remember helping him talk to producers and discuss creative issues on the show.

It was clear that my husband was already moving on with his life, even though he knew I was hopeful that we could get past these hurdles and try to keep our marriage together.

Despite all of the drama, I thought at least we'd be a family together on Thanksgiving. I pressed him to find out if he would be around for the holiday. However, his meetings, work, filming, and other business always took precedence over seeing his family. After all, we moved to L.A. without Terry. Now it was November. I guess I was just plain stupid for not seeing it for what it was. I was hopeful and trying to give him his space if that was what he needed, but enough was enough.

He told me that he was going to spend the holiday with his mother back in Florida since she was getting old. Well, in the end, he didn't even see his mom on Thanksgiving. Instead, he spent it with his buddy, and who knows who else. To his friends, it was poor Terry, all alone on the holiday, but they didn't know the real story. It was *his* choice not to be with his family on Thanksgiving.

Terry never warmed up to my family. He never realized that they were always his biggest cheerleaders, a true support system through thick and thin. They stuck by him after his affair with Kate Kennedy. They always tried to make him feel loved. But I believe underneath it all Terry felt threatened by such closeness, even from afar. He always thought they were "after his money"! It was a system of love and support from family—my family— and he was not used to that. Terry never realized how lucky he was to have my family in his life. In fact, they always tried to get me to see *his* side.

Things began to unravel further in my mind as I began to put the pieces together. Terry's choice not to be with us on Thanksgiving after all we had endured with the accident, at a time when we needed to be thankful and come together; his minimal involvement with me or the kids; threatening Brooke that if he wasn't part of her new TV show there would be no show; the fact that he owned two phones; the money in the safe; never giving me eye contact; canceling my credit cards; his sleeping apart from me both physically and sexually; constant bickering and picking fights; nasty phone calls; the mysterious blonde on the back of his Jet Ski; all the signs in Miami and his secrecy—just everything. And to think I still didn't really know about Christiane.

I was tired of the excuses. I was emotionally drained. I had hit my limit, and it was time for me to move on with my own life. I found a divorce lawyer on the Internet. I knew that I eventually had to get a different lawyer. I would need a pretty powerful attorney to go up against Hulk Hogan and his deceptive ways. However, at the time, I just needed to file the papers because I knew that it was over.

I talked to a lawyer in Clearwater. He was good enough for now. I gave him a brief description of what I was going through, filled out the paperwork, and thankfully still had a few bucks in one of my accounts to pay him the $500 retainer he asked for. He asked me where Terry would be in order to have the process server deliver the papers to him. So many thoughts ran through my head. Am I really doing this? Oh my God, what's going to happen when he gets these? Will he be sorry? Will he be angry or sad? But at that point, I knew that none of that could be the case. He was just too cold and calculating to really have any remorse or regret. I went ahead and gave the lawyer the address and location of the sound stage he was working on. I had no clue where he was staying, so it had to be at his place of business, during business hours. The papers were delivered to him at Sony Studios in Culver City, California, at one P.M. on November 20,

2007. I felt like I had a thousand pounds off my chest by just filing the papers. I didn't know how I was going to get through the divorce . . . I just knew I had to do it.

I didn't tell Brooke or Nick that I was actually filing for divorce. I needed to keep some things to myself at that point. Nick asked to go to the set the same day to visit Terry.

"Are you sure?" I asked him, trying to dissuade him from being in the path of fury.

"Yeah, Dad's doing a bunch of stunts today and I want to go see him," Nick responded.

Reluctantly, I dropped Nick off at the set that morning. Not too long after, I got a phone call from Nick. "Mom, did you file for divorce from Dad?" he asked.

My heart pounded with anxiety. "Yes, Nick. I had to."

"Oh my God, Mom. I can't believe it. Dad was shocked!" I knew Nick understood. He saw that I was miserable, sad, crying, and upset most of the time.

Why was Terry so shocked? How much more did he think I was going to take?

I ended up going back to Clearwater a week or so before Christmas 2007. My lease was up on my Los Angeles home, and I needed to get back to the house in Florida since the divorce was filed there. I had to charter a jet to fly across the country with the kids, dogs, and birds in tow. Once again, I went back to Florida.

Things were a bit different this time because Terry would end up moving out. When he found out that I was going to come back to our Willadel home, he opted not to live with me, and after Christmas, he decided to stay at the beach house. He packed some of his stuff and split. Now that I look back, I'm sure it was because he had already been dating his new girlfriend, Jennifer. He stayed with the family for a few days before moving out but slept in another room.

A few days before Christmas, I set up a tree and raced around to try to get some shopping done. The kids had been through so much over the year that I just wanted to make the holidays as nice for them as I could. They needed something happy in their lives.

On the day before Christmas, I was going to do a quick trip to Target. When I was leaving the house, I saw my sixteen-year-old dog Foxy sitting in the driveway lying in the sunshine. I couldn't take her to Target with me, so I placed her on the grass and let her sit in the sun, which she loved. Twenty minutes later, the caretaker at my house called me and told me that the carpet-cleaning van accidentally ran over Foxy and killed her. I ran out of Target hysterical, screaming in horror! I wanted to *die*! She was like my child!

I didn't even care if we had Christmas at that point, I was so devastated.

My mother tried to convince me to make a nice dinner, decorate the house for Christmas, and try to keep our family together. She felt that I should throw in the towel on divorce proceedings if Terry could give it one more chance for the kids' sake. For us, for twenty-four years! Because I was feeling so vulnerable, I thought maybe my mom was right and that maybe this was a good time to try to repair what was left.

On Christmas Eve, I spent most of the night alone in the basement, wrapping presents for the kids. I didn't want them to see the gifts before they got wrapped. I guess Terry was upstairs watching TV.

I was so tired from moving out of the California rental house, unpacking, Christmas shopping, crying every half hour over the realization that my dog was not with us, feeling like it was my fault for being in a hurry and leaving her outside, and the fact that my life was falling apart. I was trying to put on a happy face for Terry and the kids, but it was the hardest thing ever. I think at times, I was the most emotional one out of the bunch. The kids watched TV like it was old times. Terry was quiet and unemotional. I guess he was just trying to keep the peace until he could escape.

After the kids went to bed, I asked Terry to help me place the gifts under the tree. We were alone and I wanted things to just go back to the way they once were. I wished it was all a bad dream, but seeing Terry so distant I realized we might not be able to pull up the nose on this thing.

Still, I wanted to try. Once last time, I asked him if we could talk before we went to bed. We went into my bathroom— a place where we would usually go to talk. It was quiet, big, and comfortable. I asked Terry to try and make our marriage work. I apologized for everything that I had done and said. I told him that I didn't know why it was all happening, but said that I still loved him. I asked him to "please, put his ring on and stay home."

"No, I'm not ready," Terry responded. "I need more time."

Why? Don't you love me? I thought.

"You really need to think about it?" I asked. "I'm your wife. We're your family and we're in crisis right now." But I left it at that, it was Christmas Eve. He went upstairs to the extra bedroom and closed the door.

The next morning, we celebrated Christmas. Terry sat on the

couch like a stiff with fake smiles and laughter. After we opened all the presents, Terry said he was tired and went upstairs to lie down. I followed him upstairs.

"Can we please just try to work it out?" I asked. "Will you please put your ring on and just come home? I'm willing to throw in the towel. Let's try to be together. Let's make this work and start over for our kids' sake. Please? I still love you and I want to try. I'm sorry. Please?"

"I don't know," he said. "I need more time." That, along with his coldness, said it all.

At that moment I decided to take his "I don't know" as "no." To me, when you say that you need more time, you're not serious.

Terry being there for Christmas, going through the motions, was a joke! "You don't want to be together," I said. "You don't want to make this work! You have no intention to make this work, and you haven't for a long time! I'm sick of all of this!"

"You win! You win! You fucking win!" he yelled. "You filed for divorce. You win!"

At that moment, he got up and went into his bathroom. He was talking to someone very quietly on the phone. I walked in and surprised him because I wasn't in the habit of following him in there. I was pissed! Now, I *didn't* care either!

"Who's that on the phone?" I asked. "Is that your girlfriend? Do you have a girlfriend?" (I knew he did.)

"It's none of your goddamn business," he shot back. "What I do is none of your business anymore. You filed for divorce and can do whatever you want. And so can I."

He immediately began packing up his things and abruptly left for the beach house. He called me when he got there and told me that he didn't want to argue anymore. He said that he left because he was afraid I might hit him and throw things at him because I had done it before. I had *never* done that before. In fact, he was the one who did that to me! *What was wrong with him?*

My attorney told me that it looked like he was setting up a false history. Terry was just trying to provoke me to hit him, so I would get arrested. I realized that he was being closely guided by his attorneys, and everything was a strategic move.

On December 26, 2007, I was alone in my bathroom and I just started writing. As the new year approached, I needed to write how I felt after everything that happened.

> *I like my face with wrinkles and glasses. I think I still look pretty and I haven't changed for the worse with age yet. I like my light blond hair and my body. It's starting to trim down with no exercise. It must be the stress! I love my house and the property it's on. But that doesn't mean it's my home or my sanctuary anymore. If anything, my bathroom seems like it's my only place of refuge—just to light a candle, turn on some music, or read my books. To think or be with my dogs. To dream about the future and just think about the past. It's only a sanctuary when Terry is not here, because when he's around my aura is invaded. His presence is disturbing and it sidetracks me from just really relaxing. I know I can make a new home that's mine and the kids. If everything I had bottled up could just get out it would be so unbelievable what I could do. My mind has no boundaries, only my body. I am physically present, but not emotionally. I feel like a captive*

being held hostage with no reason why other than I continued to stay. Why did I stay? Kids? His image? The
TV show? I am scared of being hurt. I feel like if the
boat hadn't taken on so much water we might have been
able to weather this. I just think about the kids and how
much they need us both. Way down the road, what are
we going to do for holidays, weddings, grandchildren and
not growing old together anymore? But he doesn't look to
the future of us or our family. I want to share my life and
my kids' lives with family and friends. We're lonely. We're
trapped. We all have to "do as we're supposed to do." But
really we are just living in a communal and controlled
environment. We are all just pawns in his game of life.
I think he's got the sleeper hold on us from moving on or
doing what we want even if it's for the benefit of all of us,
until he has something going for himself. It would look
pretty bad if his son and daughter got something going
before him. Or, even maybe me. Oh, but the scale is not
tipped in his favor, for sure. And now the accident. Now,
it's really not tipped in his favor. But when you're a selfish
person you just can't see it. He's too competitive for me.
It's just constant tit for tat and counting. Keeping score.
Holding people back from the dreams that they have and
the things that they love. How long can you mask selfish-
ness? All the dirty tricks in the book come out. Shortcuts.
Cheating. Lying. Stealing. I have seen it all. I am very
aware now. I know him so well that he's very transpar-
ent to me and he hates me for it. In his desperate attempt
to maintain his position, he's gone even lower. Saying he
knows people in the Hells Angels and if I ever left him

journey is over. He has no empathy or remorse. I meet his needs, but he doesn't meet mine. Problems are never resolved. It's just over and I'm ready to move on. I'm not crying over him anymore! I shouldn't be sad because it's his loss. It gives me everything to gain. I see the situation clearly now. He broke the deal. I guess he thought I would never find out or pay attention to the obvious signs of his extramarital affairs. He lost out. Not me.

Starting Over

With Christmas over, moving back into the home on Willadel Drive again, getting all of the dogs settled, still missing Foxy, and realizing that my filing for divorce was a definite go-ahead, I had a lot on my mind for the new year ahead. Most people decide on one or two things that they'd like to see changed. I had a whole laundry list! I had stuff I had to do . . . wanted to do! Things to fix, change, replace, people to call—you name it. I had to start my life over.

The new year unfolded with the Monday after the Christmas holiday, which was the first business day between Christmas and New Year's. I needed to go talk to someone at Morgan Stanley and discuss what was going to happen to our nest egg and how to set myself up financially. I got up early, and went in to meet the new man in charge of the accounts, Travis. As we started talking, he asked me to write down the account numbers so he could quickly research them. We had so many I really had no clue. But we did have an accounting firm that handled everything for the family and our businesses. I had never met Travis before, and I'm sure he had no idea of what was going on between Terry and me, but word of my divorce was broadcast all over the news, from CNN to TMZ. Terry even went on the radio to feign shock over my filing for divorce—of course, he conveniently failed to mention his affairs, deceit, and attempt for me to sign a "midnuptial" he had hidden in documents allegedly drafted to "help" our family.

I think Travis might have been scared, not knowing how to handle my request, but I wanted to see all of the account balances and past deposits because I had the feeling that Terry may not have been depositing recent checks. I didn't know the fifteen account numbers off the top of my head . . . like who would? So I called our accounting firm, relying on the fact that they had all of them stored in their files. When I asked for the account numbers, they noticeably balked and claimed they were in a filing cabinet in a locked office. Red flag! The representative then asked me if I could call her back in fifteen minutes for the info. Instead, fifteen minutes later Travis walked in the waiting room and told me that he got a call from the accounting firm and they told him that Terry and his "lawyers" had me taken off as cotrustee on *all* of our accounts, all but the one in my name!

"What?" I said in a shocked voice. I didn't exactly know what that meant, but I had the feeling that the accounting firm was withholding information that was rightfully mine at the time. We were still married. We were still paying the firm. And they were taking sides with my husband, knocking me out of the loop! Travis explained that the accounting firm had a document that Terry and his "lawyers" prepared back in October. *October!* I thought. That meant that one whole month *before* I even filed, he removed me as a cotrustee!

My head swam. I was angry. I'd been duped. He got to the accounts before I did, not only removing me as cotrustee but transferring funds and assets into companies and partnerships that only Terry controlled. I had been taken off as cotrustee, and people whom I knew I didn't trust now had control of our life savings.

It fucking pissed me off to say the least, and I thought back to the conversation we had at Christmas where he claimed that he needed more time. More like ran out of time! There was no way he could have turned back at that point. He had already drawn his line in the sand. It made me rethink *everything* he said or did as far back as I could remember. How low would he stoop for the almighty dollar? I realized that if he had signed that document in October, then that's what he was arranging on the phone in the hallway in the hospital all day. And there I was sitting in the hospital room thinking that we were there as a unified front supporting John and his family. He must have been planning on leaving me before the accident, but now he would have to approach it differently. I started realizing that maybe he wanted to leave me first. He must have already had his next "life" lined up and was ready to make the break. I just made it easy for him . . . and harder for myself. I get it. That's why I got sent a *mid*nuptial agreement in October—oh my God, my head was reeling. The audacity of him! What about the kids? Did he even think about what they might think of him doing that—transferring millions of dollars into sleazy hands?

I knew then that the new year was going to be hell! If Terry was *this* calculating . . . well, my thoughts about how he'd treated me in Miami, the midnup, and his keeping the details of the accident from me put me in a ferocious rage like I've never been in before! I shook Travis's hand and told him I'd call him soon. Then I jumped into my Escalade and headed back home, trembling. Once in my car, I called the accounting firm again. Ironically, the representative I had tried to talk to wasn't available. My heart pounded and my head raced. I felt anger and confusion as I thought about how Terry had premeditated *all* of this. I pulled in the driveway, and the firm's representative called back. I told them how obvious it was that they had taken my husband's side, and I hung up on them. I was the outlaw and Terry was Hulk Hogan, "the icon" on television every week. It was sickening. I called my lawyer, and then I called my mom. I had no idea what to do.

When I got out of the car, sweet Nick was in the garage playing with a remote control toy he got for Christmas. Brooke was already back in Miami preparing for her new show, *Brooke Knows Best*. My lawyer told me not to freak out and he was on it. He said to just take care of my kids. I felt some relief throwing this in his lap now.

Ultimately, my first priority was Nick and John. Terry's lawyers were working with Nick concerning his liability with the accident. I wanted to talk about it with Terry so badly. I felt like this was all Terry's fault, but I couldn't ask anything.

Poor John. I felt so bad for him and his condition. All we could do was offer moral support to him and his family, going to the hospital every day and praying that he would come out of his coma. It was so scary, and seeing his family go through it was even worse. Our hearts went out to them. We needed a miracle!

Prior to the accident, I knew John well, but not his family. Basically, his mom was homeless, sleeping on a cot at the hospital. I immediately stepped in, and Terry and I leased an apartment for her and her younger son, Michael. I paid a year's rent in advance, provided furniture, and helped her get her things out of storage. I called all of my friends to help her move in, so she could at least have a place of refuge during all of this turmoil. We took food to the hospital for the family and continued to do anything possible to help. She was ever so grateful and appreciative!

A Not So Secret Admirer

Brooke's new show was beginning to tape in Miami. She needed me to pop up in the intro to the show as "Mom." In February 2008, I went down to Miami. I tried my best to keep things positive. I even brought my friend Paige down to Miami from Clearwater to help "set decorate" Brooke's new condo, something I always did with our show. Even though I wasn't going to be used on Brooke's new reality show, I didn't care. I would do *anything* to help her!

Paige and I went to Target and Walmart, looking for cute stuff to make the furnished condo that VH1 had leased look a tad bit more girly. We came back with throw pillows, candles, dishes, and rugs—all that fun stuff girls love! As we unpacked the stuff in Brooke's living room, the music that she recently recorded played on the stereo. Brooke's longtime friend Ashley, who was her roommate on the show, was there, too.

Brooke's phone rang and she told us that Christiane was coming over to help. *Awesome,* I thought. Even though I had had suspicious feelings about Christiane in the past, I'd dispelled them since she and Brooke were such good friends; I thought for sure Brooke would have had a bad vibe too if Terry and Christiane had been involved. Remember, I thought that Terry may have been interested in her, but Brooke put my mind at ease and told me, "No, Christiane's not that type! She's fine. Don't worry, Mom." We told her to stop and pick up some wine, that we were in decorating mode.

Christiane told Brooke that she didn't have a date on Valentine's Day, so she needed to hang out with the girls. I hadn't even remembered that it was Valentine's Day, and I don't think Brooke, Ashley, or Paige did, either. When Christiane showed up, she had a single long stem red rose for Brooke and a couple bottles of wine. The music played, the girls laughed, and we decorated. It was a good time.

Christiane hung out, but she hardly spoke to me and wasn't very friendly. I guess it was foreshadowing for what was to come.

The next day, I packed my things, hugged my Brookie, and wished her all the luck with the new show. She looked and felt beautiful for the first time since all of the traveling on her music tour and moving to Miami. I was so happy to see her glow! For a minute, she said she wished I could stay, but that her father was on his way down to film the first episode and was bringing his new girlfriend. I joked a bit, saying, "Oooh, Dad's still with the same girl. Could be your stepmom!"

Brooke was nervous telling me, but she wanted to be honest. I had no idea he was dating anyone that seriously yet. I mean, when did he have time for a love life with all of the other stuff going on? It kind of pissed me off that he was shoving his new girlfriend in Brooke's face so fast, especially right when she was trying to focus on her own show. It's a lot of pressure. And now this?

Brooke let me know that she didn't like the snarky comment. I apologized, kissed her good-bye, and wished her good luck. Her dad and the new girlfriend showed up later that day after Paige and I drove home to Clearwater. I guess they had dinner that night and were all preparing to film the first episode the next morning.

Well, as Brooke explained it to me, after dinner Terry and Jennifer went to their hotel and Brooke met up with her on-again, off-again boyfriend Stack$ (the music label's owner's son). He mentioned to Brooke how strange it was to see her dad with a different woman other than her mom and joked about how he was used to seeing Christiane on his arm. Brooke demanded an explanation from him. He told her that he thought she knew because everybody from the record label knew about Terry and Christiane being together the whole last year that we had all lived in Miami.

At four thirty in the morning Brooke called me, hysterically crying. "Mom, you're not going to believe this! Are you sitting down?"

"What's the matter, Brooke?" I asked, worried.

"Dad had been sleeping with Christiane the entire time our family was in Miami."

"What? How do you know?"

Brooke told me what her friend told her and how Terry broke up with Christiane before he started dating his new girlfriend.

"They broke up? How were they even dating?" I asked. "He's married! To me!"

That night, Brooke insisted that Christiane meet with her at a friend's house to discuss this affair. Christiane drove over in the middle of the night and handed Brooke a letter. It explained how she had deep feelings for Terry, how this love affair couldn't die, how she never wanted to hurt us, and so on. Brooke was devastated that her good friend could not only hurt and betray her but do the same to her family as well.

Looking back, I guess that's why Christiane didn't have a date on Valentine's Day. Come to think of it, that's probably why she didn't have a date when we all went to the Forge on New Year's Eve. I guess the suspicions I had were dead-on!

I HAD ALWAYS SENSED THAT THERE WAS AN AFFAIR GOING ON IN Miami, but I had no proof. I made my decision to divorce Terry based on the type of person he had become and how he was treating the kids and me. Finding out about Christiane was the cherry on top of the sundae. I believe if I hadn't summoned the courage to divorce Terry, and if I stayed with him, history would have repeated itself again and he would have continued to cheat.

When Brooke told me about Terry's affair with Christiane, it felt good to hear Brooke say that my suspicions were right all along. She told me that she felt bad for me. Having Brooke understand my position gave me extra confirmation that I had made the right decision.

Chapter Twelve

COUGAR UNLEASHED

HE TABLOIDS WERE RUNNING WILD WITH THE Hogan divorce. It made headlines. I was really upset about how they spun the story because it wasn't how it went down. But there was no way to change it. The kids were actually happy we were getting a divorce. They knew how miserable Terry and I both were on a daily basis.

In the months that followed after Valentine's Day, I was back in Clearwater with Nick, meeting with lawyers and discussing how we were going to move forward with the divorce. There was a lot to deal with emotionally: finding out about Terry's escapades with Christiane, knowing about Jennifer, still dealing with the accident and all the lawyers Terry had for that, and worrying about John. However, my main focus was Nick. I wanted to give him the quality of life I'd always given him, continuing to be a parent who actually watched over him. Nicky was so scared, sad, and insecure about his and John's fate.

I still had to deal with phone calls from Terry that were somewhat civil at best, with us mainly talking about the lawyers and Nick's future. Terry was careful to keep the calls short, not leaving any room for small talk about our personal lives or his past or me questioning him in any way. He seemed so matter-of-fact whenever we spoke. I never heard any emotion in his voice. He never apologized for the accident or for our twenty-three-year marriage crumbling. I guess I expected to hear a bit of remorse somewhere. Narcissist!

I began speaking up and telling Terry exactly what was on my mind on the phone and over e-mail. At this point, what did I have to lose? He was on the hook for the accident. He was guilty in the divorce for cheating. I wasn't afraid anymore, so I said how I felt. And it made me feel great. During our marriage, I was afraid of saying what was on my mind because I didn't want to have a fight. It was easier to sweep it under the rug. Now, he deserved a boatload of my opinion. I was ready to dish, but the lawyers eventually stopped me from doing that.

I was informed that Terry would only speak to me through our lawyers. *Wow, what a coward,* I thought. *He didn't just wear yellow . . . he is yellow.* I hated him for ruining our lives. He was like a hurricane that blows through leaving a path of destruction and never once looking back! As much as I wanted and tried to keep up a game face for Nick, I eventually crumbled. I think at that point I threw in the towel. I needed to take a sleeping pill and *sleep!* I let the animals be cared for by Jorge (one of the faithful helpers I had); I didn't fix my hair or color it; I didn't eat much. I cried a lot. Sometimes so much that I couldn't even fake going out without sunglasses on—my lips and cheeks were so swollen. I didn't set foot in the gym. In fact, I hated the gym, because it was full of Terry's gym equipment.

One day to try and help get myself out of the horrible depression/anger phase I was in, I decided to clear his shit *out* of the Willadel house and put it in the garage. Terry had taken most of his important belongings to the beach house where he was staying. If he didn't want to live at Willadel, fine. I went downstairs and proceeded to open every cabinet, ripping his crap from them. Brooke came in and caught me in the rage! How do I explain this to Brooke? Clearing the stuff out of the house, and my life, was cleansing. His clothes were out! I called for my housekeeper to bring me black Hefty bags, and I told her to start shoving his crap into them. I also found some of his personal things that he wouldn't be too proud of.

After I purged his closet and the house, I felt much better. One of the healing processes was to make a list of how I was feeling in my "old life" and what I wanted my "new life" to be, the life I had wanted for such a long time. *How could I achieve this?* I wondered. The first step was to write it down and visualize it. So that's exactly what I did.

OLD LIFE

- *Entrapped*
- *Lonely*
- *Sad*

- *Scared*
- *Victimized*
- *Tired*
- *No self-respect*
- *Fat*
- *Feet hurt*
- *Headaches*
- *Anxiety*
- *Shaky*
- *Unloved*
- *No gifts*
- *No special times*
- *No vacation*
- *Heart palpitations*
- *Not cherished*
- *Used sexually*
- *No communication*
- *No trust*
- *Fear for life*
- *No future*
- *No joy*
- *No peace*
- *Miserable marriage*
- *My needs not important*

New Life

- *Move to California*
- *Pretty house*

- *See family*
- *Pets*
- *New town*
- *Job in TV*
- *New gym*
- *Lose weight*
- *Hair extensions*
- *My own money*
- *My own space*
- *My own schedule*
- *New dates or boyfriends*
- *Horseback riding*
- *Travel to Europe*
- *Vocal and dance classes*
- *Shopping*
- *Laughter*
- *Freedom to make friends*
- *Take care of myself*
- *Self-confidence*
- *Feel younger*
- *Dress pretty*
- *Garden*
- *Spa trips*
- *No guilt*
- *Decorating*
- *No more self-destruction*
- *No more breakdowns*

I realized that I needed to quit wallowing in my own self-pity and let go of some of the anger, at least for Nick's sake.

I just got tired of crying.

As Nick awaited his trial, I often took him to the beach. I wanted him to do the things that kids do for a change, instead of him being with his dad, who always tried to treat him like a grown man ahead of time. Nick was seventeen years old at the time of the accident. Kids don't need to ride around in a boat full of beer hunting for chicks. Nick needed to go bowling, go-cart racing, skateboarding, riding bikes, and so on.

On May 9, 2008, Nick was to appear in court where a judge would determine his fate. I was scared for him, myself, and our family. We tried to have some fun that weekend before the pending court appearance. That Friday afternoon Nick, his friend Danny, and I hit the beach. On our way back home, I saw a group of guys hanging out by our beach house. In our area of Florida, the guys weren't too attractive, usually a bunch of families with kids or senior citizens. One of the guys in the group was a pleasant surprise! He was tall and tan and had an amazing build. Whoa! I asked Nick to check him out and see if he was as cute up close. Nick was fine with me asking him to do that. He knew that his dad had cheated on me. He knew I was alone all of those months and how sad and lonely I had been. He knew it was time to step out of the shadow of the old life and move forward. After the guys talked for a few minutes, they waved me over. The guy's name was Charley Hill, and he was gorgeous for sure—beautiful white teeth, eyes as green as the Gulf of Mexico, and cute feet!

I told Nick to bring the guys down to the beach house. I didn't really think about it as a date. When they showed up, we sat in the backyard on the beach. Charley had blond hair covering his chest, arms, legs (and head). Terry used to shave his whole body because, truthfully, he's really hairy. And it's dark hair. So seeing a man with sexy blond hair all over his bod was a turn-on. I like a man to be hairy. And shaggy blond hair on his gorgeous head! Wow, I just wanted to run my hands through it! He had a beautiful smile—something about his little overbite, and big white straight teeth, and the way his top lip looked when he smiled— that was sexy! His friends were tan and beachy, too. There were a couple of younger guys and one older guy with him.

Charley said he was twenty-three. Sure, he was young, but I wasn't looking for a long-term thing at that moment. It had been almost a year since I had even slept with Terry. *I am not dead yet,* I thought. Terry's not crying in his soup! I felt it might be good for me to move on. When I saw another man and realized that if I wanted to, I could go for it . . . it was liberating. I was single and could date again. And I'm sure Charley was feeling what I was feeling. There was definite chemistry there. I mentioned how tan he was, looking at his tan feet and his cute toes! (With me, guys have to have a cute face and cute feet. Whatever, that's my thing.)

I asked what he did and he told me that he was home from college and was working at a nearby Jet Ski rental concession for the summer. He said that he went to college on the east coast near Daytona Beach. He was a springboard diver on the team preparing to go to the Olympics. I learned he placed fourth in the nationals and was on a scholarship for his diving. I was dumbfounded! He was definitely no beach bum. In fact, he was also attending the firefighters' academy. (Well, he certainly lit my fire!)

Charley laughed easily—a free spirit—and he had cute smile lines around his clear green eyes. He's an old soul, and I'm young at heart. It was weird flirting with another man at first. It didn't feel wrong, though . . . not now, and I needed to follow my heart (which was pounding in my chest). It was like a guilty pleasure, because I was not completely divorced; in my heart, I felt because I had two kids, it would probably be better to have my divorce final before I started dating. Then again, I started looking around and reading the tabloids and seeing all these other people who had left their husbands or wives, dated other people, and had babies before they were even divorced. Terry was already on to his second girlfriend (at least she was the second that I knew of). *What am I, chopped liver?* I thought. *Why can't I have someone in my life who makes me happy or I could laugh with?*

So Charley and I ended up chitchatting on the phone. I felt like I was in high school with a crush. Even though I was excited that I'd met someone so nice, I needed to focus on Nick's court hearing.

My mother decided to fly in that weekend for moral support. On top of it, it was Mother's Day weekend! All I wanted was to hold Brooke and Nick tightly in my arms and never let go of them. I knew Brooke was a big girl, filming her own show in Miami, but I wasn't used to not having her around. She was my little girlfriend. And Nick was my baby. However, the family dynamics had already been changing when we were living in Miami. Both kids were living their own lives. Their bedrooms were on the other side of the house, and I was already used to them not being right there under my feet. I wasn't physically seeing them around all of the time, and it was really difficult.

Nick was scared, upset, and sad. He feared for John's life. They were best friends and it was an accident. The reality show depicted Nick as a wild child. That really wasn't the case. He was a soft, mild-mannered, intelligent, and caring individual. Nick was not a reckless person. I think he was judged improperly due to the character he played on the show. The thought of him facing John's family, the judge, the press, and the flurry of allegations against him was overwhelming.

We entered the courtroom to a barrage of cameras. Terry would not speak to me, because his attorneys advised him not to. I am sure he was fine with that. He didn't have to explain himself to me about the accident or his actions, cheating on me, any of it. I couldn't get an answer out of him for anything. How convenient for him!

The verdict was one that we didn't want to hear, and after months of Terry's and Nick's lawyers telling me that Nick wouldn't do time, he was sentenced to six to nine months of jail—solitary confinement. They handcuffed him, fingerprinted him, and took his coat; and two deputies walked my baby out of the courtroom—right then and there before the whole courtroom, tons of cameras, and, of course, John's family and his mother, Debbie. Brooke was white as a ghost. My mother sobbed hysterically. And Terry sat there with a stone face, watching them take his son into custody. I looked at Nick, trying to be strong for him. I blew him a kiss and looked him in the eyes lovingly, knowing that it would have been easier if they would have just shot me. His eyes were on his mom. As he disappeared around the corner, I looked over at Terry. He couldn't look any of us in the eye! He stared down, as his lawyers surrounded him in a protective manner and walked him out, as if he was "too" bothered by it. My God! All I wanted to do was share a glance with him, to realize the despair we were feeling as parents, but nothing. No communication, no hugs, no emotion . . . nothing.

As we walked out of the court building to the parking lot, the mob of press surrounded Terry and his team of lawyers. Was he sorry? Was he sad? Who knows? In a time like that, families usually come together no matter what! I felt like his guilty conscience got the best of him though. Was this karma for all of his misbehaving? His self-serving ways? I felt and still feel none of this would have happened if he was "aware" and "present" as a parent and husband instead of worrying about when his next piece of ass would be.

Terry's limo pulled around and he went home to Jennifer. Brooke got in her car and left for Miami. My mom and I left and headed for the airport. It was the worst day I've ever had.

I hugged my mom good-bye, trying to act strong so she didn't worry about me, although she knew, as a mother and a woman, the agony and loneliness I was experiencing.

After I dropped her off, I began to sob as I tried to drive home. The closer I got to home, the worse it got. I couldn't contain it anymore. I walked in the back door, crying and alone. All of my dogs were around me, and I think they sensed something was wrong, too. Usually, their cute little faces could take me out of any bad mood. But nothing could save me from the pain that I was feeling at that moment. The house was dark and no one was there. I walked through the once-happy kitchen where Nick, John, Brooke, and all the kids congregated. I looked across to the living room, seeing the sofa that Terry sat on. The pictures of the family, Terry's office, Nick's bedroom, Brooke's bedroom— quiet, dark, still. There was no one at home, and no one would be coming home. I looked at my pack of dogs following me, minus one—Foxy. I never even made it up to my room. It was just too much. I crouched to the floor, sobbing inconsolably.

I sounded like an animal in pain, wailing a type of crying I had never experienced before. *How could God be so cruel?* I wondered. *He can give and take, I guess, but all at once?* Everything was so out of control, so bad, I really didn't think as a mother I could survive another day of the pain.

I didn't even know how I was going to take my next breath.

My husband, my kids, my dog, John, the legal battles—it was just too much to bear.

In a moment of insanity I ran out the back door crying. I couldn't even see through the makeup in my eyes. I got into my Mercedes and just drove. I had no idea where I was going. I just headed south and while driving over a bridge I was thinking of just driving off it! I didn't want to kill myself and die. I thought about my kids. And my family who I knew loved me. I knew I had a purpose in life. But, at that moment, I didn't know how to live, either. I didn't know how to go on. I didn't know if my car would go off the bridge at that point or I'd drive in front of an oncoming truck.

My phone rang as I approached the bridge. I looked at the caller ID through my tears and it read: Charley. It was a total surprise. We hadn't spoken since we first met. I was very concerned about what Nick was going through. I had already made up my mind that Charley was kind of young and, while it was a real turn-on, with all of this pressure going on it was hard to think about my love life. I decided to put it on the back burner. It was fun for that day, but I wasn't even sure if I should see him again.

I decided to answer. Charley asked me why I was crying. He told me not to drive and to pull over and catch my breath. Charley saved me from my insanity at that moment.

I went back home and slept. The next day he called me at one P.M. in the afternoon, and I agreed to meet him at the beach. I felt I needed to be around somebody and have some positive energy in my life. It was great to have a reason to leave and somebody to meet up with.

Charley was a lot of fun and a great listener. For being so young, I was surprised that he was such a heartfelt and emotional guy. We ended up hanging out at the beach that day, and I saw him every day after that. I would ride my bike while he rode his skateboard. He was just the type of carefree fun I needed.

I wasn't really worried about how Nick felt about my relationship with Charley because he was with me the day I met him. Charley was sweet and charming and Nick and I liked him. Quite frankly, Nick was concerned about my welfare and happiness, and being with Charley made me happy. Who's to say what's right or wrong in this day and age anyway. Nick was very mature and optimistic about my future. When I went to visit Nick in jail, he asked me if I had hung out with Charley again. I told him that I did and that although he was young, we got along great. On the other hand, I think that Brooke was a little shocked and surprised to find out. She wasn't living with me at the time and hadn't really seen what I had been going through. I think with mother/daughter relationships it's hard for a daughter to see her mom sleeping with anybody besides her dad. I'm sure Brooke wanted to see me happy, but I think that maybe she thought that I was just with Charley as revenge. I wasn't.

I latched on to Charley and he basically never went home. I didn't want to be alone, and I loved being with him. We talked and cuddled. And, yes, we slept together! When we did, it was an emotional awakening. It was the first time I had slept with someone besides my husband in twenty-four years and I was scared, but he was amazing in so many ways.

I felt guilty for being with someone different, but I had no idea why. Was I crazy? My husband was already living with another woman! In fact, when I filed for divorce in November 2007, I hadn't slept with Terry since July of that year. That was his choice. So it had been ten months since I had had sex, and it was about time I got with somebody; Charley was the man!

I was nervous when we made love for the first time. He had a young, cute, tight buff body and long gorgeous legs! He was kind and loving. It was really exciting to be with someone new and fun and somebody who actually had sex back with me!

CHARLEY AND I STAYED IN FLORIDA, AND ON MAY 31, 2008, OUR relationship became public.

It happened in Las Vegas at the Palms Place Hotel and Spa, where Terry and I had a condominium that we had bought as an investment. The owner, George Maloof, had invited the celebrities who purchased penthouses in the building for a red carpet event that May. Last minute, Terry wanted nothing to do with it and was willing to let it go. Everything was still in litigation, and we didn't know what the fate of the condo was going to be. George's publicity people asked me to come. I said sure.

I didn't want to go alone and I decided to take Charley. I stayed close with one of Nick's friends, Ray, who used to be his hockey coach, and his wife, Lisette. I asked them to come along as well. When we arrived in Las Vegas, they showed us to the condo that we had purchased. The party was on! The condo was beautiful, big, and on the fifty-fourth floor!

It was the first real fun I had in so long. I was around true friends. We had the red carpet event to attend, and Charley looked gorgeous. We bought his outfit at the last minute in Vegas. It was all really exciting. I wore a Roberto Cavalli dress and when Charley and I stepped onto the carpet, he proceeded to step on the train of my dress, ripping it. Uh-oh! I was having so much fun that it didn't matter. He was such a good-spirited guy. We went behind the curtain and actually stapled the big wad of fabric back on to my dress. And the show went on!

I grabbed Charley, they opened the curtain to the red carpet, and away we went! Reporters and photographers were yelling, "Linda, Linda, Linda! Who's the guy?" I was overwhelmed. They asked Charley if he was dating Linda Hogan and he responded, "We're just chillin'." At that time, we didn't know what we were ourselves. We were together for sure, but to what extent we didn't know. We hit the dance floor and had a ton of fun, mingling with other celebrities, including Ashlee Simpson, Pete Wentz, Janet Jackson, and Verne "Mini-Me" Troyer. I was loving life again!

The photos from that red carpet are still gracing the tabloids to this day. That night made news and changed history. It changed my life because it officially made me a cougar, which is a term I'd never even heard of before. It put Linda Hogan on the map with my own identity. It was really a positive step for me because being in the spotlight on my own and not being on Terry's arm, having recognition for my own life and new positive choices, was exciting. The tabloids blew it up that I had a boy toy. At that point, Charley had to come clean and tell me the truth and that he wasn't really twenty-three; he was almost twenty (that meant nineteen). I told him I was cool with it, as long as that was the real truth. He was legal and that was all I knew. As surprised as I was about his age, the truth was that I was already crazy about him and falling in love.

Kiss My Glass

Terry now knew that I had a boyfriend—a much younger lover—and he was very bent, pissed, and jealous. Brooke was deep into shooting her show and spent a lot of time with her father because he was on the show with her. Terry was subliminally brainwashing Brooke about how evil I was and how wonderful he was. And, of course, what a wonderful person Jennifer was. He basically took Brooke's eye off the ball, making her think that he was this upstanding individual dating a nice "flight attendant" like Jennifer and I was dating this young kid. Terry made Brooke forget that he had been sleeping with her young girlfriend the whole year before this, and wasn't exactly coming clean about Jennifer's past, either.

I think Brooke didn't know what to believe anymore. But she also knew she had to stay tight with her dad or she didn't have a TV show. I suppose she thought it was easier to distance herself from me and work with her father. It was very hurtful. And to know that she was this innocent person who was being manipulated by Terry the whole time angered me even more. She was my flesh and blood. My best friend. I don't know what Terry said to her at the time, but he tried to turn her away from me.

She told me that she would never hurt me. It was a confusing time.

Over the next two years as my divorce was being finalized, Terry would taunt Charley and me, annoyingly accusing us of things publicly in the media. He used every dirty trick in the book, including trying to create a false history of drug and alcohol abuse for me.

My lawyers had already informed me that Terry was out to get me. They told me to mind my p's and q's and to be careful. I was very cautious. That's why one night when I went out for dinner with our hairdresser (she did Terry's hair extensions too!), I didn't drink.

When I left the restaurant, I made a wrong turn due to some road construction as I made my way to the highway. I got pulled over and there was not one, not two, but three cop cars at the scene, they also sent a DUI enforcement car conveniently at the same time! Lights, sirens, the whole nine yards. This was obviously a shakedown.

The police took me to the parking lot of a nearby mall where they tried to break me down. They proceeded to put me through a DUI test, and I passed with flying colors. They also searched my car and purse for no reason whatsoever. I didn't even know what my rights were. I had never gotten a DUI or been searched. I only allowed them to search my car and purse because I had nothing to hide. I remember the captain saying to the cop who was trying to break me down that they had to let me go. He was really pissed. Afterward, I called my dad and told him about what happened and he said that this was definitely *not* normal police protocol.

As I drove home I realized that Tracie, the hairdresser, was probably trying to set me up. Throughout the evening, she kept going to the bathroom to talk on the phone because she said she had no reception at the table. But my cell phone worked fine when I took two phone calls from Brooke. The hairdresser was probably talking to Terry on the cell phone in the bathroom. She also kept trying to get me to taste her martini and take some pills she offered me. I believe she was trying to get me intoxicated; I didn't fall for it. Eventually, Terry even used my hairdresser against me in court. Talk about split ends!

On another occasion, after I had flown back to Los Angeles by myself, I was approached by two alleged undercover officers as I got off the plane. They asked if I was Linda Bollea and I said yes. They explained that they wanted to speak with me in private. My heart started pounding because I thought they were going to tell me that something had happened to one of my kids. I couldn't understand why else they'd be confronting me.

The officers told me that they had reasonable cause to believe that I had narcotics on me and that they were going to search me and my bags. This was absolutely ridiculous because I didn't use drugs. They were waiting for a female assistant and a room, which meant they were going to do a cavity search. When they said that, I felt that this was all set up by Terry. He loved to embarrass me, and this would have been his crowning glory, to have me busted at LAX airport; with TMZ and the paparazzi, it could have been a field day for the press. Oh well, sorry to disappoint! I made a call to my lawyer, Ray Rafool, and within moments, they released me, because they did not really have proof. Like that! I have to say that my divorce was getting to be a three-ring circus.

Gold Digger?

During the two years of a stormy divorce, Terry called me a gold digger, but the only ones getting rich were the lawyers! And I had one brilliant lawyer to his team of six or seven!

Terry used publicity to paint the picture from his perspective, and I never had a platform to speak. My lawyer kept telling me not to say anything back. From daily radio to tabloid headlines to threatening to pull an O.J. stunt, I wished I had had someone to help me! I knew that winning the court of public opinion would be tough against an icon, especially in his hometown where he was loved. His best friend had his own radio show there, which was broadcast nationally. Terry had his own private and exclusive national megaphone, which he could use to say anything to America (though he admitted that not everything he said on the show was true; it was "entertainment"). Huh! At my expense! Terry was also friends with all the locals, and the neighbors took his side. Terry was a national icon. Strangers rolled their eyes when they saw me, like *I* was the town whore, when truthfully, it was Terry! *Still,* no one really realized that I had left because of his cheating!

During this time, Charley and I were laying low. Every dime I spent was being monitored by Terry's lawyers and mine. You know, he was so worried about *me* spending *his* money. *Hello?* We had been married for twenty-four years (well, one month short of twenty-four) when I filed for divorce, and we earned it together! No, I didn't wrestle, but I did everything humanly possible to keep the loose ends tight—kids, house, you name it! I don't have to tell all of you behind-the-scenes spouses! I'm sure you know there was a hell of a lot more going on behind the scenes. But he hated the thought of paying me alimony to support what he claimed to be a "flamboyant" lifestyle. Yeah, my so-called jet-set life of going to court and the beach, and taking care of my dogs.

Thank God I had Charley. This encouraged me at the time to make a list of all the things I was thankful for in my life. *Thank you, Lord,*

- *For Nick being alive.*
- *For John being alive.*
- *For a strong relationship with my kids.*
- *For my sister, brother, mother, and father.*
- *For a strong and loving family to support us.*
- *For a beautiful relationship with my parents.*
- *For the patience to stay as long as I could.*
- *For my true friends: Jeanette, Paige, Beth, and Jill.*
- *For Brooke, her health and safety, her future that you are guiding her with your love.*
- *For my dogs and pets that love me back so much.*
- *For the guardian angels that surround my children all the time; I know they are there.*
- *For making me beautiful inside: kind, giving, loving, honest, and with a conscience.*
- *For the wisdom to know that I need to move on.*
- *For the strength to decide being alone is a better choice now, even feeling the fear and being strong enough to endure the change.*
- *For a second chance to find someone who really loves me.*

- *For my health now, even though I put myself last,*
  but I will be strong now for you and my kids.

During that time, the lawyers had arranged to give me a base amount per month to live on. No problem except that I still had bills, which most months exceeded the full amount I had to operate with. I luckily had money that was in a trust in my name alone, so I delved into that savings account to survive. That was all that I had access to because Terry (and his friend Eric Bischoff) had virtually every penny under his control or the accounts were frozen by court order. I had a mere fraction of our megadollars. So needless to say, the lifestyles of the rich and famous were curtailed.

I'm a simple person at heart. That served me well because most women in my financial category would curl up and die once their funds were reduced. They don't know how to survive the cut! Sure, at one time it used to be Neiman's. Now I think twice before I go to Target or Walmart. There were no more fancy restaurants. All we did was ride bikes, or hang out on the beach. When we were home, we grilled burgers and played with the dogs.

Clearwater is quite different from L.A., and everyone there is very simple. I grew up that way and raised my kids that way, so I was used to it. I had a lot of great new friends that I had met through Charley who were his age, my age, and in between. Just nice people. We had a karaoke machine in my kitchen along with a disco strobe light. The weekends would be a 1980 revival! Jill and Paige and Beth—backup singers!

Charley was a big help then, too. He helped me "trim the fat" so to speak (in more ways than one!). Yes, I lost weight, probably from having to be naked in front of a new guy, but that's not what I mean. He helped me by realizing it was okay to enjoy the simple things in life. He liked getting outside and just existing. He made me realize that I don't need to dress up, go somewhere, or spend money to have a nice life. We went to all the little beach hangouts and friends' homes, and we walked the dogs and gardened. I loved it. It was actually an easy transition. Realizing that you can have a completely functional life on a budget is okay. It's good. It makes you reevaluate things, people, places, and yourself! You are forced to see the world in a pure way. It makes you more creative.

The sad part about my relationship with Terry was that not only had he been living a secret life away from me, but he physically couldn't do anything with me except go out to eat. Because of all his injuries that led to surgeries (hip and knee replacements, a bad lower back with compressed discs, fifth vertebrae with bone spurs), the poor guy was always in pain. He broke his ankle years ago, too. I was tolerant about all of his physical disabilities and helped him deal with them for years. I felt bad about all he had to deal with from the life of wrestling. It was hard work, so I excused him for a lot because I felt sorry for him. But with his wasting money and infidelities over the last few years leading up to our split, I just wasn't as sympathetic anymore. And I decided it was time to stop with the excuses!

I was always physically active—running every day, keeping up with my kids, skating, biking, swimming, skiing, weight training. I also loved to dance. But I was doing it alone. I couldn't do those types of activities with my husband or plan any kind of vacations where we went hiking or skiing. We couldn't ride Harleys together anymore. (Yes, I ride my own bike. Years ago,

Terry bought me a Harley, and I learned how to ride in front of our house.) As time went on, he couldn't do very much with me anymore. So I just stopped planning activities together because I felt bad doing them without him.

With Charley, I can be active again. Every year since the divorce, I take a trip to the mountains with him. I feel like I have a new lease on life. I used to panic if I had a bad e-mail or a situation like the car breaking down. I don't let it ruin my day anymore. Things do have a way of working out for the best. Trust that! When you are fifty-one years old, you have to look at life more calmly. I'm a mother, daughter, sister, and girlfriend. I'm a catalyst for so many people, and I have to be a good example and a role model: realizing this has really helped me.

The last deposition in our divorce (not in my post-divorce cases to force Terry to abide by the marital settlement agreement he made) was a deposition of Charley. *What did Terry hope to learn?* I wondered. He didn't learn anything. But it was his way of applying pressure, putting fear in me that Charley might spill his guts. What he and his lawyers didn't realize was that there was nothing to spill! Nothing that they could ask Charley that would scare him. The only thing threatening that day was Terry's presence—six feet seven inches, three hundred pounds, with black sleazy shades on the whole time *inside* the office. The depo began: Spell your name. Where do you live? How old are you? Where do you work? Obviously, Charley was nervous sitting across the table from Terry, his three lawyers, the court reporter, me, my lawyer, etc. Charley tried to act composed, but he was stuttering slightly, shaking a bit, spelling out his full name. Don't forget, I'm sure that all Terry was thinking was that this young cabana boy was sleeping with his wife! But as the questions continued, Terry asked to take a break.

He walked out into the lobby. Charley left to go to the bathroom. My lawyer and I went outside as well.

As my lawyer and I walked back inside the building, to our surprise and shock Terry and Charley were standing together in the doorway area, talking civilly! This was *not* status quo for any deposition. Then Terry called me over. He told me that he was over all the bullshit and that he didn't want Charley to fear him and his presence. He wanted to stop the deposition and come to a mediation. *What?* I thought. *Why the sudden change?* I'll never know. Maybe it was because Terry realized that Charley had been dragged into this. Or maybe Terry had ulterior motives to end the divorce drama, because he finally had a deal, a business deal that would require his time and that it would behoove him to just move on. I don't know, but two days later we met again. This time it was just me, Terry, my lawyer, and three or four of his attorneys.

For the first time in a long time we talked amicably. We began to negotiate. Back and forth we went, until we shook hands on it all. I hugged Terry, thanked him, and told him I still loved him! His change of heart made everyone there so happy. You felt a lightness in the room. While everyone was shocked, they were also so relieved about the change of attitude. Truth is, no one likes to see people fighting and at each other's throats. And it was like old home week! Outside the room, I hugged his lawyer, he hugged me, Charley and Terry patted each other hug style on the back. Crazy! Just insane! And, like that, it was over.

Life in the Jungle

Building a marriage and a life with someone is like building a house of cards. It has to be treated very delicately. Every time you build up a wall you intend for it to be strong. But sometimes the weight becomes too much on one of the sides. Then it all comes crumbling down. That's what happened to me.

I was spent mentally, physically, and spiritually. And when these three parts of your life, which are supposed to work in unison, are failing, it's time to make changes.

We all have awakening moments during our lives. For me, it was right before I decided to divorce Terry. One day I realized that I wouldn't let anyone hurt my heart this much. At first, I was angry. Then I felt powerless. Next all the animosity, anger, rage, resentment, and fury that I had been building up came out of me at once! I knew I needed to save myself, but I just didn't know how. There's an old saying, you can't eat the elephant in one bite. I learned that the only way you can truly find the peace you are looking for is in baby steps. I understand it now.

After reading this book, if you realize that you're faced with a situation like mine, don't feel that life is over. This is a fresh start for you. You should be excited! Build a new life for yourself. Take it from someone who has been in your position. I couldn't see the light at the end of the tunnel. I want you to know, there is an end to the insanity. And the time it takes to get there goes by faster than you think it will. Get out of that jungle like the lioness (or cougar) that you are!

Here are a few little pointers I felt helped me and hopefully can help you, too! I'm not a psychologist. I'm only speaking from my heart and using the knowledge I've gained through my experience as a wife, a mother, and a survivor of divorce.

Make a list: Make a list of everything that is negative and keeping you from the life you want. Then, make a wish list of everything you dream of. Start crossing stuff off those lists. Before long, you'll be where you want to be!

Take care of yourself: It doesn't mean that you have to go to a fabulous salon. It could mean getting a little bit more sleep, taking a walk, or taking a few vitamins. You don't feel so insane when you've given yourself time out of the busy schedule.

Start living: Be more adventurous! Say yes more often. Sometimes, it's just easier or more convenient to say no, but you know what they say, "Nothing ventured. Nothing gained." So go for it!

Your inner circle: You need a support system of close friends around you at this time. Being alone is dangerous. There are friends and family near you or a phone call away who really do care about you. You can lean on them, but don't abuse their support. Allow them to make you feel better and laugh a little.

Action causes reaction: When you smile at a random person, they usually smile back. It changes the course of your day. Go for that dinner with that friend. Do take that dreaded phone call—grab the bull by the horns and handle that situation. Good or bad, things will change! If you are monopolized by fear, nothing will change.

Forget crying: Crying in your soup, feeling sorry for yourself, is natural and you deserve to feel sad. But after a while ask yourself: Is he really worth me crying *this* hard? Swollen eyelids and cheeks weren't my best look. Kick it in the head and get over it!

Don't use your kids: Don't use them as shrinks, pawns, or excuses. Keep them busy—let them go to Grandma's or a friend's house. It's better for them not to be dragged into the divorce and not to see Mommy or Daddy as a mess.

Stay classy: Don't act on emotion and impulse. Even though you want to prank call him, egg his house, put a tuna sandwich under the hood of his car. Oh, I can think of lots of things that I wanted to do. Three words: *not worth it!*

Redecorate: I found it so healing to go around the house removing his "stuff." Make the space *yours,* even if it means less is more. Flowers, a few inexpensive items from Walmart—throw pillows, a new bedspread is a must! Remove draperies. Open it up then have a party!

Silence is golden: It's so hard to stay quiet, but by gabbing to your neighbor, the gardener, or others about the details of your new private life, they're sure to reach the ears of your husband's camp. The less said, the better.

Payback: Even if you think that sleeping with his boss or best friend would really fluff his feathers, you'll regret it. Having him seeing you happy is enough payback!

Pity party: Don't go on and on about your divorce at a party. Leave people wondering how you manage to stay so positive and look so happy. Fake it till you make it!

Young and restless: I pulled my bike out and started riding it again. I played outside with my dogs. I walked on the beach. I stayed up and sang karaoke in my kitchen with a disco ball glowing, all alone till midnight! I tried on my short dresses with heels and modeled for myself in my bathroom mirror (looking at the bright side, not the backside). I felt empowered, young, beautiful, and *sexy!*

Live in the now: Be aware of your surroundings, of your health, of your youth of today. Enjoy it. Tomorrow will have its own complexities, so be present in each moment. When your kids are talking, listen and be there. My ex had tattoos put on each wrist. One says "Aware" and the other "Present." He's probably wishing he'd done more of that during his marriage. I guess we all need reminders of how important it really is.

Seeking closure: Hopefully, you'll find a few tips in my book to help you with this. You can't ever expect full "closure." With kids, families, legal tugs-of-war that never seem to end, you may never get it. Just realize that your new life is all the closure you need!

EPILOGUE

*T*ODAY IS JULY 21, 2010. I'M IN NAPA VALLEY! MY
goodness, I've dreamed of taking a trip up
here for the longest time. Me being from California and loving
wine, nature, and good times, I had to pinch myself as I sat
back in the velvet easy chair on the Sonoma County Wine
train. I was actually there! Not dreaming about going there.
I brought Charley and my darling Brooke! (She's twenty-two
now!) We are all happy, laughing, and enjoying the day. Brooke
has known how much I used to talk about a trip like this,
and I never realized I'd actually *be* on this trip and enjoying it
with her. Charley is laughing, Brooke is taking pictures, and
I can't help but reflect—I take a sip of my delicious sauvignon
blanc and gaze out at the vast open vineyards, the beautiful
green hillsides, the sun-drenched skies in the warm California air.

It's been a long road getting to this point. During my marriage, we had good times. I was a full-time support system to my
husband, but with a lot of hard work came exciting times, too. I
was more than a wife; I was a mom, friend, adviser, housekeeper,
party planner, sex goddess, chief cook, and bottle washer. I wore

just about every hat. I loved my life and thrived on being a multi-tasker. I handled it all with ease; the only thing I couldn't handle was Terry's infidelity—again.

I had some tough years throughout my marriage and always tried to see the glass half full. But through the divorce, it became so difficult to keep the same perspective. At times, I thought there would be no end to the pain of understanding what my marriage was really about, no relief from the sadness, no escape from the reality of realizing your family is broken, your husband of almost twenty-four years is gone—crying as you start packing your life into cardboard boxes, thinking that the road ahead is unbearable, not knowing where or how you will end up.

I'm thankful to God and my family, children, friends, and Charley for surrounding me with their help to weather the storm. But I did it and you can, too. God closes doors, but he opens windows. You need to look at your life at a low point and view it as the beginning, not the end. A second chance to live and love again your way! Be a little kinder to yourself. Instead of the regular old to-do list, make it a "to-do-for-me" list. Write that "bucket list" down, even if it seems like you're a zillion miles away from doing or achieving any of it. Just write it down and date it. Start saying yes a bit more, and stop taking life so seriously and smile more. When you're independent, these things radiate positivity. You need strength of character to become a survivor. This is only the beginning of a new you!

ACKNOWLEDGMENTS

I want to thank all of the people who helped me come to the realization that I needed to write this book. Many of you encouraged me before I ever put my pen to paper by having faith in me and helping to see me through such a difficult time. I'm thankful to have you all in my life!

Brooke and Nick, being your mom is the most joyous thing in my life. Thank you for your love, your kisses, and your respect. You are the wind beneath my wings. P.S. I miss making you chocolate ba-bas!

Charley, for always being there for me through the public and private times in my life, loving me and my kids, giving me a future to embrace, making me laugh, hearing me cry, and loving life with me.

My family, who has always been a phone call away and has always been there for me. My mom, for her unwavering support and love; my dad, for being a good dad and a good husband to mom; my sister, Christie, my confidante and shrink; and my brother, Joey, for fixing up all my homes and adding a little humor!

Ray Rafool and Ivan Parron, for being the smartest, most

savvy lawyers in the world! Travis, for helping me deal with the financial confusion I was in during my divorce. My closest friends, who listened to me cry, made me laugh, and always believed it was "Linda Nation." Jorge and Veronica, for taking care of me, my house, and all the pets through this ordeal. Thank you.

Lisa Sharkey, Amy Bendell, and the rest of the team at HarperCollins, for believing in this Valley girl with a story. My book agent, Frank Weimann at the Literary Group International, it's time to celebrate over that bottle of super Tuscan. My photographer, Navid Matoory, for shooting a fantastic cover.

The Hyatt in Westlake Village, California, where I sat for hours writing and rewriting this book. Thanks for the service with a smile and a great chicken Caesar salad.

Foxy, my beloved little dog, who after her death became my little guardian angel. She always protected me on earth and now is guiding and watching over me from heaven. Everything is good because she still looks out for me. I miss you.